AF574130

2016 Hurting Moms, Mending Hearts – Daily Encouraging Words

By Cathy Taylor

ISBN 978-0-9903190-9-2

Printed in USA by: **SQUARE TREE PUBLISHING** - Los Alamitos, CA 90720

Cover Design by: Cathy Nelson Arkle - The Thumbprint Group

SQUARE TREE PUBLISHING
Los Alamitos, California
squaretreepublishing.com
info@squaretreepublishing.com

Some of the darkest times in my life were during the years that I was a Hurting Mom. I was often paralyzed with fear and anxiety and it was out of desperation that I turned to the Bible. I discovered that the promises in the Scriptures were like a balm to my aching heart and the comfort I found there kept me coming back for more. I was always amazed at how quickly I received relief for my pain as I read.

I learned through reading my Bible that I didn't have to carry the burdens of anger, resentment, fear, anxiety, guilt, and shame by myself. I discovered that I had a savior, Jesus, who could and would comfort me and give me peace even in the midst of the chaos. Scripture taught me about surrendering my daughter to the God who created her and loves her more than I do.

This book contains some of the Bible verses that I clung to when I felt hopeless and alone, along with some of my thoughts and an action item for each day.

My prayer is that reading these words of encouragement will give you courage and strength to navigate through the uncertainty of what each day may bring.

With a Mending Heart,

Cathy Taylor

DAY 01

"He heals the brokenhearted and binds up their wounds."

Psalm 147:3

As a Hurting Mom, we often feel as though our hearts are breaking into a million pieces. It is difficult to see past our pain and we isolate and lose sight of the good things in our lives. This verse tells us that we can rest in the assurance that God is in the business of healing and He can and will take care of us in the midst of our pain.

Today let's choose to trust that God will carry us through our pain.

DAY 02

"The God of all grace, who called you to his eternal glory in Christ, after you have suffered a little while, will himself restore you and make you strong, firm and steadfast."

1 Peter 5:10

The heartache that we are experiencing will not last forever, but God will use what we are going through to strengthen us.

As we draw closer to Him we begin to rely on Him for our peace and comfort, and we learn to trust Him with our wayward child. This verse tells us he has called us to his eternal glory and that our suffering is just for a season. It's so great to know that God will not leave us in this place of pain, but that He, Himself will be the one to restore us.

Find one way that you can draw closer to God today.

DAY 03

"Cast all your anxiety on him because he cares for you."

1 Peter 5:7

Anxiety is such a prevalent emotion when we have a child or children who are making bad and damaging choices in their lives. There is nothing worse than being tied up in knots because we are anxious. God wants us to let Him take that anxiety from us because, just as we love our children, He loves us. As we learn to surrender to Him it becomes easier to trust Him with our child, and the weight of what we are going through becomes lighter.

Give your anxiety to God and allow Him to comfort you today.

DAY 04

"Do not fear, for I am with you; do not be dismayed for I am your God. I will strengthen you and help you; I will uphold you with my righteous right hand," says the Lord.

Isaiah 41:10

We sometimes feel overwhelmed and paralyzed with fear for our child. We wonder where they are, if they are safe, and if they will ever turn around. God's Word tells us that we don't have to be afraid because He will give us what we need to get through this time. We are not alone! He will hold us up when we feel as though we can't make it through another day. He is with us every step of the way.

Take comfort in God's presence throughout your day.

DAY 05

Jesus said, "Peace I leave with you; my peace I give you. I do not give to you as the world gives. Do not let your hearts be troubled and do not be afraid."
John 14:27

Peace seems to be so elusive when we are worried about our child. However, God wants to give us the perfect peace that only He can give. In fact, He is waiting to do just that. The secret to receiving His peace is to focus on Him instead of on the chaos, uncertainty, fear, and anxiety that are taking over our lives because of the choices of our child.

When you find yourself in the midst of chaos today, turn away from it and focus on the Lord.

DAY 06

"Be strong and courageous. Do not be terrified; do not be discouraged, for the Lord your God will be with you wherever you go," says the Lord.

Joshua 1:9b

It sounds good, doesn't it? Be strong. Be courageous. Don't be terrified or discouraged. It's much easier said than done. Discouragement and fear seem to have taken up permanent residence in us. But then we get to the last part of that verse, "GOD WILL BE WITH YOU WHEREVER YOU GO!" We are not alone. He is with us. We can do this with His guidance, love and support.

Seek Him and He will be the one to give you the strength and courage you need to make it through this day.

DAY 07

"We wait in hope for the Lord: he is our help and our shield."

Psalm 33:20

We don't have to wait for our child to turn around and make right choices in order to experience relief from our pain. If we place our hope in what our child is doing or not doing we will be sorely disappointed. We quickly learn that our help will not come from outside sources. Our hope is in the Lord and what He wants to do with us. If we allow Him to, He will be the one to help us and protect us from the hopelessness we feel.

Let God shield you from the pain today.

"See, I am doing a new thing! Now it springs up; do you not perceive it?"

Isaiah 43:19a

There is something so encouraging about those words. We are more than ready for something new to happen in our lives. It sometimes seems that the life has been sucked out of us and we feel old, tired and weighed down. But God tells us that He is doing something new even though we might not be able to see it yet. It is exciting to realize that God is continuously working to make changes in our lives and in the lives of our kids.

Believe these words and watch for it because He is working behind the scenes in ways that we can't imagine.

DAY 09

"Praise be to the Lord, to God our Savior, who daily bears our burdens."

Psalm 68:19

Sometimes we hold on so tightly to the pain, worry, anguish and anxiety that we are carrying around with us that we forget to allow God to help us. In this verse we are reminded that we can let go of these burdens because He wants to bear them for us. Remember to praise Him, even in the midst of your struggles, and you will be surprised by how much lighter you feel.

Pay attention to the things you have to be thankful for today and praise God for them.

DAY 10

"Come to me, all you who are weary and burdened, and I will give you rest."

Matthew 11:28

REST! That sounds wonderful, doesn't it? There is nothing more debilitating than feeling tired and weary all of the time. Not only is it hard to sleep because we are worrying about our child, but the anxiety and stress of the situation weigh us down throughout our days in everything we do. Jesus tells us that He will give us rest, even while we are still experiencing the pain of having a wayward child. All we have to do is "come to Him".

Take a few minutes right now to hand your burdens over to Jesus, the One who loves you and loves your child more than you can imagine.

DAY 11

"Then you will know that I am the Lord; those who hope in me will not be disappointed."

Isaiah 49:23b

As Hurting Moms, many of us have put our hope in our child. We hope they will come to their senses and come home, we hope that they will realize the damage their actions have caused, we hope that they will stay sober this time. Putting our hope in our child has disappointed us over and over again, but in this verse we read that if we put our hope in the Lord we will not be disappointed. Putting our hope in Him means that no matter what happens with our child, we will be alright. It means that our comfort, our peace, and our strength come from Him.

In what ways can you find hope in Jesus today?

DAY 12

"In your anger do not sin. Do not let the sun go down while you are still angry."

Ephesians 4:26

Anger is a secondary emotion to hurt. It is a natural reaction for us to lash out in anger when we are being hurt by our child or anyone else, for that matter. The reality is that when we are angry it is way more damaging to ourselves than it is to anyone else. Try to find a way to diffuse your anger before you say or do something that you will regret. One way to do this is to pray.

Talk to God today and ask Him to take away your anger.

DAY 13

"Let the beloved of the Lord rest secure in him, for he shields him all day long."

Deuteronomy 33:12b

You are the beloved of the Lord! He loves you so much that he wants to protect you from the negative emotions you are experiencing, the ones that are robbing you of peace and joy and rest. He will shield you from the pain, the guilt, the anxiety, and the fear today if you will allow Him to do so by surrendering your child and yourself to Him. Once you surrender you will receive the rest you are seeking.

What can you do today to "rest secure" in the Lord?

DAY 14

"But now you must also rid yourselves of all such things as these: anger, rage, malice, slander and filthy language from your lips."

Colossians 3:8

Anger, rage, malice, slander and filthy language will keep us in turmoil and cause a wedge between us and God. These things, for many of us, come much more naturally when we are hurting than do kindness, gentleness, love, peace or joy. However, as we seek relief from our pain by drawing closer to Jesus, we begin to move away from the negative responses that we have had in the past. Although we, alone, are powerless to control our negative responses, with Christ's help we can rein it in and respond in a way that glorifies Him and promotes positive communication.

Seek to be Christ-like in how you respond to your child today.

DAY 15

"But as for me, afflicted and in pain – may your salvation, God, protect me."

Psalm 69:29

Although we are in a lot of pain, it is important to remind ourselves that God can and will save and protect us from the heartache we are experiencing. We are so consumed with our child that we sometimes can't see beyond them and what they are doing. But, if we can just take the focus off of our child and place it onto the Lord, for even a little while, we will find relief.

Find some time today to turn your attention to God, allowing Him to comfort you.

DAY 16

"My comfort in my suffering is this:
Your promise preserves my life."

Psalm 119:50

In the midst of our pain and suffering God's promises can be our lifeline. When we feel like giving up because it's just too painful, His loving kindness will be our comfort and our strength. Throughout the Bible we are reminded of His faithfulness and as we seek Him we experience His strength and love – just like He promises! God is our life preserver and during this time we need to cling to Him for dear life.

Spend some time looking for the promises of God by reading His Word today.

DAY 17

"The Lord himself goes before you and will be with you; he will never leave you nor forsake you. Do not be afraid; do not be discouraged."

Deuteronomy 31:8

Fear and discouragement are two of the emotions that we, as Hurting Moms, live with every day. We are constantly afraid for our child because of the lifestyle he or she is living. We get discouraged over and over again because it seems like things just keep going from bad to worse. This passage reminds us that no matter how alone we feel, the Lord is with us and He promises never to leave us.

Take heart in that knowledge and rely on Him to get you through another day.

DAY 18

"Why, my soul, are you downcast? Why so disturbed within me? Put your hope in God, for I will yet praise Him, my Savior and my God."

Psalm 42:5

Our sadness and feelings of hopelessness take root deep in our souls. It seems that they are always there preventing us from enjoying our other relationships, eating away at us as we go to work each day, when we come home at the end of the day, and while we are in our beds trying to sleep. We have tried to get a handle on it, but still we remain downcast and broken. If we make time to praise God for the good things in our lives, the sadness and hopelessness we feel will begin to be replaced by a new hope in God.

Think about something good in your life and take time to thank God for it today.

DAY 19

"When I am afraid, I put my trust in you."

Psalm 56:3

Putting our trust in the Lord is a choice and a process that takes time and practice. When we get caught up in being afraid for our child we have to remember to surrender our fear along with our child to Him. Sometimes we have to do this many times a day, but over time it gets easier and soon we are able to go for a few hours or even an entire day without being consumed with fear.

Make the choice to trust God for today and when He doesn't let you down today, it'll be easier to trust Him again tomorrow.

DAY 20

"I sought the Lord, and he answered me; he delivered me from all my fears."

Psalm 34:4

God is always pursuing us. We are His children and He loves us, just like we love our kids. However, it is hard for us to hear His voice and to allow Him to give us freedom from our fears if we are not actively seeking Him. There are many ways to seek God. Of course, we can seek Him through prayer and reading the Bible, but we can also seek Him in nature or even by sharing with a trusted friend. God will find ways to speak to you, but you have to be listening.

Spend some time today seeking the Lord.

DAY 21

"Do not be anxious about anything, but in every situation, by prayer and petition, with thanksgiving, present your requests to God."

Philippians 4:6

There is nothing worse than the sick feeling we get in the pit of our stomach when we are feeling anxious about our child. How comforting it is to remember that in every situation God hears us when we come to Him in prayer. When we pray it is important to express our gratitude for the good things in our lives as well as to present our requests. God is good and if we take a moment to be thankful for what He has done for us and what He has given us, it will help us to move away from our anxiety and fear.

What are some things for which you can thank God when you go to Him with your requests today?

DAY 22

"When anxiety was great within me, your consolation brought me joy."

Psalm 94:19

God can and will console us when we are anxious. We often make the mistake of looking for relief by tracking our children or trying to fix and control them. The real answer to experiencing joy is to engage with our Heavenly Father, allowing Him to comfort us. He is the one who will give us relief from our pain. He alone can restore the joy in our lives that we are looking for.

Recognize and acknowledge your inability to control your child today, and then seek your comfort and consolation from God.

DAY 23

"Cast all your anxiety on him because he cares for you."

1 Peter 5:7

Our God is entirely big enough to carry all of our anxiety. In fact, He loves us so much that He wants to do that for us. That we are loved so deeply by the God of the Universe that He will gladly carry our burdens, is almost too much for us to comprehend. But, it's true. All we have to do is hand our anxiety over to Him so that He can replace it with a sense of peace.

Make the decision right now to allow God to carry any anxiety you may be feeling today.

DAY 24

"In you, Lord, I have taken refuge; let me never be put to shame; deliver me in your righteousness."

Psalm 31:1

Sometimes the shame we feel because of the behavior of our child causes us to isolate. We feel all alone and it seems like everyone else has perfect children while ours is out of control. However, when we can see ourselves as God sees us and as we begin to accept the fact that He loves us, we can rest in Him as we allow Him to deliver us from our embarrassment and shame.

Take refuge in the Lord today. Let Him deliver you from your shame.

DAY 25

David cried out saying, "My guilt has overwhelmed me like a burden too heavy to bear. Lord, I wait for you; you will answer, Lord my God."

Psalm 38:4, 15

There is nothing heavier than the burden of guilt. As we examine the behavior of our child we wonder, "where did I go wrong" "what could I have done differently"? We decide that it must be our fault and the guilt that we feel can be overwhelming sometimes. But, just like He did with David, when we cry out, God will answer us and give us relief.

Cry out to God if you are experiencing guilt today and then wait in confidence for Him to answer.

DAY 26

"Do to others as you would have them do to you."

Luke 6:31

Sometimes we lash out in anger toward our child because they are hurting us. Our pain makes us want to hurt them too. But, the Bible tells us to treat others (including our kids) the way we want them to treat us. Perhaps following the simple guideline in this Scripture can be the beginning of some meaningful communication between our child and us.

What is one thing you can do for your child today that you wish they would do for you?

DAY 27

"Do nothing out of selfish ambition or vain conceit. Rather, in humility value others above yourself, not looking to your own interests but each of you to the interests of the others."
Philippians 2:3-4

Have you hurt anyone as you have dealt with your heartache over your child? Have you blamed someone else for what is going on? At some point we have to put aside our own pain and focus on making amends for the hurt or damage that we have caused. Once we face our part in any broken relationship, we can begin to experience freedom.

Take time today to think about how your attitude or behavior may have hurt someone else and make a plan to ask for forgiveness.

"I have not come to call the righteous, but sinners to repentance."

Luke 5:32

Sometimes we get so wrapped up in thinking about the actions of our child that we lose sight of the fact that we too have sin in our lives. We desperately want them to repent, or turn away, from the things they are doing or the way they are living their lives. But what about us? Are we without sin?

Think of some things that you need to repent of today and ask God to forgive you. Once you do this you will begin to experience some of the peace you have been longing for.

DAY 29

"Instead, speaking the truth in love, we will grow to become in every respect the mature body of him who is the head, that is, Christ."

Ephesians 4:15

When we are talking with our child we usually feel that we are speaking the truth. But are we speaking the truth in love? Does the tone of our voice and the words coming out of our mouth indicate kindness, gentleness and love for our child? Is it evident that we have their best interests in our hearts? Or are we speaking the truth in the form of nagging, chastising, criticizing, or condemning? As we grow in our relationship with Jesus we will begin to display some of His characteristics which indicate love in its purest sense.

Make a conscious effort to speak the truth in love to your child or another member of your family today.

DAY 30

"Therefore encourage one another and build each other up, just as in fact you are doing."

1 Thessalonians 5:11

Do you know another mom who is hurting over their child or children? This verse reminds us that it is important to encourage one another. No one can encourage a Hurting Mom like another Hurting Mom. Only someone else who is going through the same pain and heartache can truly relate to another who is experiencing the same pain.

If you know another Hurting Mom, reach out to her today. This can be done with a phone call, a note, or even a text. It will bless not only the mom you reach out to, but it will bless you too.

DAY 31

"I prayed for this child, and the Lord has granted me what I asked of him. So now I give him to the Lord. For his whole life he will be given over to the Lord."

1 Samuel 1:27-28a

Our kids have never belonged to us. God created them and gave them to us to take care of for a little while, but ultimately they belong to Him. The problem is that we often want to hang on to them, forgetting that God is in control and we are not. We feel that we need to orchestrate the consequences of their decisions when, in fact, God has things to teach them. How many times are we, as moms, the ones who get in the way of what God wants to do in our child?

Spend some time thanking God for your child today and then surrender Him or her to Him. Ask for His help to get out of the way so that He can do what He wants to do in their life.

DAY 32

"God will grant them repentance leading them to a knowledge of the truth and that they will come to their senses and escape from the trap of the devil, who has taken them captive to do his will."

2 Timothy 2:25b-26

Most likely our child is not going to come to a knowledge of truth because of our scolding, nagging, criticizing, or because of the threats we make. It is only going to be through God's leading that they "come to their senses." What we can do is stand in the gap for our children and pray for them.

Today focus your prayers on asking God to stir in your child a desire to repent and that He would lead them to a knowledge of the truth about who He is and how much He loves them.

DAY 33

"Pray without ceasing." (KJV)

1 Thessalonians 5:17

Prayer doesn't always have to be as formal as bowing our heads, folding our hands, and closing our eyes. We can pray wherever are and whenever we want. Our prayers can be as short as one sentence, or even one word, while being aware of the presence of God and knowing that He hears us. Prayer without ceasing is about an ongoing conversation with God, just like we would have with anyone else with whom we are spending time.

Throughout this day remember that God is with you and He is listening to you. Go ahead, whenever you have a thought about your child, direct it to Him.

DAY 34

"'For I know the plans I have for you', declares the Lord, 'plans to prosper you and not to harm you, plans to give you hope and a future.'"

Jeremiah 29:11

We spend so much time thinking about and worrying about the "plan" for our child that we often lose sight of the fact that God has a plan that He wants to carry out in us. He wants us to have hope for our future, no matter what our child is doing or not doing. And best of all, His plan is not only for us to have hope and a future, but His plan is for us to prosper as well.

Ask God to show you what His plans are for you. Ask Him to give you the hope that He talks about in this verse.

DAY 35

"And the God of all grace, who called you to his eternal glory in Christ, after you have suffered a little while, will himself restore you and make you strong, firm, and steadfast."

1 Peter 5:10

For some of us it feels like we have already been suffering for a long while, doesn't it? The thing is that God deals with eternity so even our entire lifetime on this earth is just a little while to Him. Holding on to this promise that God is going to restore us and give us the strength to remain firm and steadfast in Him reassures us, even in the midst of our suffering.

Spend some time today focusing on what it means to you to be restored by God.

DAY 36

"They celebrate your abundant goodness and joyfully sing of your righteousness."

Psalm 145:7

We spend a lot of time lamenting about the pain we are in and focusing on the negative things that are happening because of the decisions of our child. This verse reminds us that even in the midst of the mess we can find evidence of God's goodness. Our spirits will be lifted if we celebrate even the subtle signs that God is with us.

Find one thing that you recognize as God's goodness in your life and celebrate it by thanking Him.

DAY 37

"Let us not neglect our meeting together, as some people do, but encourage one another, especially now that the day of his return is drawing near."

Hebrews 10:25a (NLT)

Sometimes the burden of guilt and shame that we carry are so great that we begin to isolate from others. We don't want to be around people who seem to have perfect kids. We don't want to answer questions about how or what our child is doing. However, it is important that we get together with people we trust, people that will support and encourage us through this difficult time of our lives. God did not create us to be alone. We need each other.

Make a plan today to get together with someone who will support and encourage you. Put it on your calendar.

DAY 38

"Arise, cry out in the night, as the watches of the night begin; pour out your heart like water in the presence of the Lord. Lift up your hands to him for the lives of your children, who faint from hunger at every street corner."

Lamentations 2:19

How many nights have you lain awake worrying about your child? Instead of lying there worrying and feeling overwhelmed with anxiety, pour out your heart to the Lord. Get up out of bed, raise up your hands and pray for your child and for yourself. Express your worries and your frustrations, your anger and your disappointment and then surrender your pain to the God who is right there with you and loves you so much.

Make a commitment today to turn your worries into prayers of surrender.

DAY 39

"A gentle answer turns away wrath, but a harsh word stirs up anger."

Proverbs 15:1

It's pretty hard to be gentle when we are dealing with a child who is breaking our heart. Anger is a secondary emotion to hurt or pain and our natural reaction is to lash out. This verse tells us that responding to our child, or anyone else for that matter, with harshness only perpetuates the inability for helpful communication.

If you have an opportunity to respond to your child today, try to do it gently. Or maybe it is a spouse or another family member that is in line for a harsh word from you. Ask God to soften your heart and give you words and a tone of voice that will not alienate those you love.

DAY 40

"For all have sinned and fall short of the glory of God."

Romans 3:23

Sometimes we get so focused on the sin of our child that we lose sight of the fact that we are sinners too. This verse says that ALL have sinned; not some, but ALL. We may be so caught up and focused on what we perceive to be the sins of our child that we are overlooking the things in our own lives that we need to work on.

Spend some time today figuring out what areas of your own life you need to work on with God's help.

DAY 41

"Trust in the Lord with all your heart and lean not on your own understanding; in all your ways acknowledge him, and he will make your paths straight."
Proverbs 3:5-6 (ESV)

Relying on our own understanding instead of trusting the Lord's infinite wisdom can leave us with feelings of emptiness, bitterness, and fear. We fear for our child, we fear for the future, and we fear that we will never have relief from the ache that we wake up with every morning. But the Bible promises that when we turn our thoughts to God and seek His plan, things will start looking up and our fear will subside.

Commit to acknowledging God in every decision you make today. Let Him direct your path throughout the day.

"As a mother comforts her child, so will I comfort you," says, the Lord.

Isaiah 66:13

We experience a great deal of pain as we become aware that our child no longer desires comfort from us. Our identity is in our motherhood and being a nurturer and comforter has been our role for such a long time that we may not even know how to receive the comfort that God wants to give us. How long has it been since you have allowed someone else to comfort you?

Start today to allow God to comfort you in the same way that you have comforted your child.

DAY 43

Jesus said, "In this world you will have trouble. But take heart! I have overcome the world."

John 16:33b

Trouble is not what we signed up for when we became a mom. This is not the way we imagined things would be when we held our precious baby for the first time. However, this verse shows us that trouble in this world is to be expected and we don't get to choose what shape or form it comes in. The good news, as Jesus reminds us, is that He has overcome the world and He can help us move away from our pain.

In what ways can you begin to allow Jesus to overcome the trouble in your life?

DAY 44

"Praise be to the God and Father of our Lord Jesus Christ, the Father of compassion and the God of all comfort, who comforts us in all our troubles, so that we can comfort those in any trouble with the comfort we ourselves have received from God."

2 Corinthians 1:3-4

As God comforts and heals us and we begin to experience His peace in our lives, we can offer comfort and hope to other moms who are going through similar situations. We may not feel like we have anything to offer someone else, but the truth is that simply sharing our story about being a Hurting Mom can give comfort to someone else who is in the same situation.

Reach out to a Hurting Mom today. Share your own experience with her and let her know she is not alone.

DAY 45

"God did not give us a spirit of timidity, but a spirit of power, of love and of self-discipline."

2 Timothy 1:7 (NLT)

On our own we do not have the strength or the self-discipline to surrender our kids. Every minute we are fearful of the consequences of what they are doing or what they might do. However, God, in His infinite love and goodness, gives us a spirit of power that allows us to make the tough decisions and the strength and self-discipline to follow through with the things we have to do for our own preservation.

Reach out for and accept these gifts from God as you navigate your way through this day.

DAY 46

"The Lord your God is gracious and compassionate. He will not turn his face from you if you return to him."

2 Chronicles 30:9b

Sometimes we feel that we have traveled so far from God that there is no way that He will hear us or answer our prayers. This verse reminds us that God is a loving God, full of grace and compassion. He will never turn away from us and He wants to help us, and all we have to do is turn to Him.

Take a few minutes today to commit or recommit to spending time with God every day in order to build your relationship with Him.

DAY 47

"The Lord stilled the storm to a whisper; the waves of the sea were hushed. They were glad when it grew calm, and he guided them to their desired haven."

Psalm 107:29-30

As Hurting Moms we are in the midst of a storm that seems like it will never end. Even if our child is still acting out in self destructive ways, God can and will calm the storm that rages within us. He will take away our anxiety and the pain we have in our hearts if we let Him be the one to guide the way we respond to our child.

Ask God to calm your storm and allow Him to guide you today.

DAY 48

"I praise you, Lord, because I am fearfully and wonderfully made; your works are wonderful, I know that full well."

Psalm 139:14

When we are carrying around the weight of guilt and shame because our child is not "perfect" like everyone else's children seem to be, it's hard not to feel like a failure. When we get down on ourselves we need to remember and believe this verse that tells us that our loving Father made us fearfully and wonderfully. He is a good God and He doesn't make mistakes.

Think of some of the good things about you that God has made and praise Him for them.

DAY 49

"We have put our hope in the living God, who is the Savior of all people, and especially of those who believe."

1 Timothy 4:10b

If our hope in life is tied up in trying to control our children to be the way we think they should be, we will probably be sorely disappointed. Our hope has to be in God! He is the one who will save our kids as well as the one who will save us.

Today focus on shifting your hope to the God who loves you and loves your kids more that you could ever imagine. Begin to let go of the idea that you are going to be the one to save your child.

DAY 50

"I will heal my people and will let them enjoy abundant peace and security," says the Lord.

Jeremiah 33:6b

What an incredible promise this is! Do you long for peace and security? Do you want to experience healing? Allow God to heal you the way He promises He will. Open yourself up to the peace and security that He wants you to enjoy. Sometimes we think we have all the answers and we get in the way of the healing that we seek and that God wants to do in our lives and the lives of our kids.

In what ways can you "get out of the way" of what God wants to do today?

DAY 51

"Above all else, guard your heart, for everything you do flows from it."

Proverbs 4:23

As Hurting Moms we tend to harden our hearts in order to protect ourselves from feeling the pain. Guarding our heart does not mean to harden it, which causes us to miss out on the good things in life. It means to protect it so that we can continue to experience life to the fullest, even in the midst of the pain. God can and will protect our heart if we ask and then allow Him to do so by focusing on Him instead of what our child is doing or not doing.

Ask God to help you to guard your heart so that you can enjoy life today.

"The joy of the Lord is your strength."

Nehemiah 8:10b

How long have you been allowing the actions of your child to rob you of joy? When we don't have joy we feel weak, unmotivated and sad. When we are finding our joy in the love and goodness of the Lord, regardless of what our child is doing, we experience the strength we need to move through the day. Remember we don't have strength on our own. It is the joy that we find in the Lord that will give us strength.

What can relying on the joy of the Lord help you accomplish today?

DAY 53

"Everyone should be quick to listen, slow to speak and slow to become angry, because human anger does not produce the righteousness that God desires."

James 1:19b-20

For some of us, speaking comes much easier than listening - especially when we are angry. When something happens to make us mad we tend to immediately lay into whoever is making us angry. Listening is something we have to decide to do, and sometimes it is a struggle, but you'll be amazed at how quickly your anger will fade into the background when you take a moment to listen before you speak.

Today make the conscious decision to practice listening before you speak, especially in those times when you are feeling angry.

"The Lord says, 'My Presence will go with you, and I will give you rest.'"

Exodus 33:14

Do you ever wonder if you will ever be able to simply rest again? God promises that He is with us and He will handle all of the things that are preventing us from resting. We won't find it on our own, but if we slow down and allow Him to, He will give us the rest we are seeking. He is the one who is actually in control of all the things you have been trying in vain to control and He is always present with you.

Take some time to "rest in the Lord" today.

DAY 55

Jesus said, "If you believe, you will receive whatever you ask for in prayer."

Matthew 21:22

You may have been praying for your child for so long with no apparent results that you feel that God does not hear you and you have given up praying. The truth is that He does hear you, but God's timing is not our timing and He is accomplishing things that we do not understand. We have to hang on to promises like this one and believe that our prayers will be answered – in His time and in His way.

Think about some times that God has answered your prayers and commit to trusting Him again.

"May the God of hope fill you with all joy and peace as you trust in him."

Romans 15:13a

We may have made the decision to trust God with our child but as a Hurting Mom we haven't been able to experience joy or peace yet because our child has not taken steps to turn their life around. This verse reminds us that as we trust Him, God wants to give us joy and peace, even in the midst of the pain.

As you put your hope in God today, open yourself up to the joy and peace that He wants to give you.

DAY 57

"Everything that was written in the past was written to teach us, so that through the endurance taught in the Scriptures and the encouragement they provide we might have hope."
Romans 15:4

There are so many wonderful stories in the Bible that teach us about God's love, goodness and faithfulness. There have definitely been Hurting Moms since the beginning of time, starting with Eve when her own son, Cain, killed his brother, Abel. As we read the Scriptures we can see how God has redeemed, restored and reconciled over and over again throughout time.

Find a story in the Bible that resonates with you and think of the ways in which it gives you hope in your own situation.

DAY 58

"In the morning, Lord, you hear my voice; in the morning I lay my request before you and wait in expectation."

Psalm 5:3

Expectation! Wait! Those are the key words for today. We request safety and restoration for our child as we surrender them to God and we pray for our own healing and peace. Then, we wait in expectation for God to act. Expect God to do something bigger and more wonderful than you could ever imagine! Be patient. Don't put a time limit on it. God is at work, even when you can't see it.

What big and wonderful thing would you love to see God do in your life?

DAY 59

"The Lord is with you when you are with him. If you seek him, he will be found by you."

2 Chronicles 15:2b

Sometimes we feel so alone on our journey as a Hurting Mom. We feel like even God has turned His back on us because we can't seem to sense Him. The truth is that just as we tend to isolate from other people in our pain, sometimes we often try to isolate from God. This verse tells us He is always with us, but it also reminds us that we must actively seek Him in order to experience Him.

Spend time today seeking the Lord through nature, prayer, or reading the Bible.

"Though I walk in the midst of trouble, you preserve my life."

Psalm 138:7a

Do you sometimes feel like you just cannot go on another day with the pain and anxiety that you feel? Does it seem that the life is being sucked right out of you by the actions or absence of your child? There is no doubt about it, you are walking in the midst of trouble every day if you are a Hurting Mom. The good news is that God is ready and willing to preserve your life.

Reach out for the Lord, your life preserver. He will be faithful in getting you through another day.

DAY 61

"Let us then approach God's throne of grace with confidence, so that we may receive mercy and find grace to help us in our time of need."

Hebrews 4:16

One of the definitions of GRACE is "unmerited divine assistance." God is waiting to assist us with our heartache over our child. The pain we are in can feel like a heavy weight that we carry with us every minute of every day. The burden of that weight prevents us from experiencing other relationships and it zaps all of our energy so that we are too exhausted to do anything else. This verse tells us that we can approach God with confidence and he will help us so that the weight becomes lighter and we can begin to enjoy the good things in our lives.

Approach God with confidence today and allow Him to assist you with your burdens of pain and sorrow.

DAY 62

"But as for me, I watch in hope for the Lord, I wait for God my Savior; my God will hear me."

Micah 7:7

It feels like all we do is wait! Many times while we are waiting we begin to lose hope and we question whether or not God even hears us because we are not receiving the answer we are looking for. This verse tells us not to lose hope because God will hear us. God truly is our Savior and as we watch and wait for Him we must continue to have hope because without hope everything seems futile.

As you wait on the Lord today ask Him to restore your hope.

DAY 63

"Devote yourselves to prayer, being watchful and thankful."

Colossians 4:2

Sometimes we are so consumed with and focused on what our child is doing or not doing that we overlook the prayers that are being answered. We have a hard time recognizing the positive things God is doing around us. As you devote yourself to praying for your child don't forget to pay attention to, or "be watchful" for the prayers that are being answered along the way. You will be strengthened and encouraged.

Watch for one answer to prayer today and thank God for it.

"The Lord has done it this very day;
let us rejoice today and be glad."

Psalm 118:24

It feels nearly impossible to rejoice in anything when we are paralyzed with hurt and fear because our child seems to be spinning out of control. But we all have good things in our lives as well and by disciplining ourselves to look for something that is good in each day, we will begin to realize that we actually can rejoice and be glad – even in the midst of our pain.

It becomes easier with practice, so give it a try. Find something to rejoice about today.

DAY 65

"Come near to God and he will come near to you."

James 4:8a

We spend so much time praying for our child, begging God to change them, open their eyes, bring them home. But how much time do we spend simply drawing near to Him, seeking His will for our own lives, sitting quietly in His presence. We are His child and He loves us just as we love our children and He wants us to come near to Him just as we long to have our child come near to us.

Spend time simply drawing near to God today.

DAY 66

"In the same way your Father in heaven is not willing that any of these little ones should perish."

Matthew 18:14

Those were the words of Jesus when He was talking about a man who owned 100 sheep and how he left 99 of them on the hills to search for one that was lost. He was speaking in a parable to illustrate how much God loves each one of us. Think about your child being the one that is lost and take heart that God is not willing that he or she should stay lost. He is seeking ways to find them and bring them home. At the same time He is not willing for you to be lost in pain and heartache.

Allow yourself to "be found" by God today. Draw close to Him and let Him comfort you.

DAY 67

"Love the Lord your God with all your heart and with all your soul and with all your mind and with all your strength."

Mark 12:30

These were the words of Jesus when He was asked which of the commandments is the most important. It's pretty hard to be loving God this way when most, if not all, of our time and energy is spent thinking about and worrying about our child. He said to love Him with ALL of our heart, soul, mind, and strength. When we seek to love Him this completely, everything else begins to fall into place and we begin to experience life again. There is nothing we can do about what our child is doing or not doing, but we can focus on and strive to love God above all else.

Spend some time today loving God with all of your heart, soul, mind and strength.

DAY 68

"My soul is weary with sorrow; strengthen me according to your word."

Psalm 119:28

Is the sorrow and grief that you are experiencing over your child causing you to feel weary, tired, and beaten down deep in your soul? This Psalm reminds us that spending time in God's Word will strengthen us and lift our spirits. Seeking comfort in the Scriptures will lessen our sorrow, help to alleviate our weariness and give us the strength to get through another day.

Spend some time in your Bible today seeking encouraging and strengthening words from God. Allow His words to comfort you in your time of sorrow.

DAY 69

"The Lord is full of compassion and mercy."

James 5:11b

Sometimes it seems that no one else understands or cares about the ache we carry in our heart because of the actions or attitude of our child. In those moments when we feel totally alone and isolated from the rest of the world, we can remember and be encouraged that God does understand and He does care about us and our pain. He has compassion for us and if we are consistent in reaching out to Him we will begin to experience His mercy in new ways.

What are some ways you have already experienced God's compassion and mercy in your journey as a Hurting Mom?

DAY 70

"But the plans of the Lord stand firm forever, the purposes of his heart through all generations."

Psalm 33:11

We may not see it now, but God does have a plan for our children as well as a plan for us. Sometimes, we, the moms, are the ones who get in the way of God's plan for our child. We undermine His plan by becoming rescuers instead of trusting Him to teach them in His own way. This verse tells us that His plans stand firm forever so eventually they will be fulfilled. The sooner we get out of the way and let God work, the sooner we will realize freedom from our heartache and pain.

Let go of your fear and surrender your child today to the God who loves them and has a plan for their life.

DAY 71

"The Lord is good and his love endures forever; his faithfulness continues through all generations."

Psalm 100:5

Sometimes it is hard to sense the Lord's goodness or His love. We have suffered for what feels like a very long time because of the actions of our children and we become disheartened. We may have lost hope that things will ever change, but this verse reminds us that God is faithful through all generations. His goodness and love endure forever and we can be encouraged as we remember that He loves and is faithful not only to us, but to our kids as well. Things might not change or get better as fast as we wish they would, but God's timing is perfect and we have to trust Him and His faithfulness for the outcome in our particular situation.

Think of some ways in which you have already experienced God's goodness and love?

DAY 72

"I pray that out of his glorious riches he may strengthen you with power through his Spirit in your inner being."

Ephesians 3:16

We get to the point where we are weak with grief, sorrow, anxiety, and fear. We have allowed our child's actions to sap the life out of us and we don't how we can possibly make it through another day. One of the ways we can pray for ourselves and for each other is to ask God to strengthen us with His super natural power. God is rich in patience, kindness, goodness, and love and we can tap into those things which will give us the strength we need to keep going.

Today spend some time praying for and opening yourself up to God's goodness and love. Allow them to strengthen you.

DAY 73

Jesus said, "Do not let your hearts be troubled. Trust in God, and trust also in me."

John 14:1 (NLT)

To say that our hearts are troubled is an understatement for most Hurting Moms. It is our hearts that are so deeply affected when we have children who are making choices that have the potential to destroy them. In this verse, Jesus Himself reminds us that we can do something about the pain we have. He tells us to trust Him. The more completely we trust Him the less our hearts will be troubled.

Focus on trusting Jesus with your child today and experience the relief that only He can give.

DAY 74

"But those who hope in the Lord will renew their strength. They will soar on wings like eagles; they will run and not grow weary, they will walk and not be faint."

Isaiah 40:31

When we put our hope in our own ability to fix, control or change our child it can cause us to become very weary, and it depletes our strength. God wants us to place our hope for our child in Him, and once we do that, we feel our strength return and the weariness is replaced by energy and joy.

Focus on getting out of the way and allowing God to work in the life of your child, and be aware of the energy and strength you will receive from Him.

DAY 75

"Blessed is the man who perseveres under trial because, having stood the test, that person will receive the crown of life that the Lord has promised to those who love him."
James 1:12

What we are experiencing with our child is a trial! The Bible tells us that if we love God and we persevere in trusting Him, He will fulfill His promise and we will experience the riches of a life that is centered in the joy and peace that we can find only in Him.

Turn your focus away from your child and put it on loving and trusting God today, and begin to recognize the joy and peace that He will give to you.

DAY 76

"But encourage one another daily, as long as it is called 'Today', so that none of you may be hardened by sin's deceitfulness."

Hebrews 3:13

Do you know another Hurting Mom? It is easy for our hearts to become hardened as we try to cope with our pain over the sin of our child. We get so caught up and feel so alone in our pain that we forget that we are not the only one hurting over our child. No one can encourage or comfort a Hurting Mom like another Hurting Mom. Who else really knows what they are going through?

Reach out to another Hurting Mom today. Let her know she is not alone in her suffering.

DAY 77

"Let the peace of Christ rule in your hearts."

Colossians 3:15a

We have allowed our anguish over our child to rule our hearts, our minds, and even our bodies for so long that we have forgotten that the peace of Christ, which is way beyond anything we understand, can and will override our pain if we will open ourselves up to it. It is up to us to make the decision to allow the peace of Christ rule in our hearts. He is ready and willing to give us peace. We just have to ask for it and then open ourselves up to receive it.

Spend some time today consciously allowing the peace of Christ to permeate your heart, mind and soul.

DAY 78

". . . to be made new in the attitude of your minds; and to put on the new self, created to be like God in true righteousness and holiness."

Ephesians 4:23-24

Do you need an attitude adjustment? When we are in the midst of the mess with our kid it is easy to become resentful and bitter. This verse reminds us that we are created in God's image and bitterness and resentment are not part of who He is, or of who He created us to be. Changing our attitude is not something we can easily do on our own, but He can help us become "new in the attitude of our minds".

Ask God to help you with your attitude today. Ask Him to help you weed out the bitterness, resentment, and other negative emotions that are interfering with you being the person He created you to be.

DAY 79

"You will call, and the Lord will answer; you will cry for help, and he will say: Here am I."

Isaiah 58:9

How many times do we cry out for help but forget to wait for or notice an answer? This verse tells us that the Lord WILL answer. He says, "Here am I", in other words He is right there with us. But we are often so wrapped up in our child and the ways they are hurting us that we overlook Him. We fail to notice that He is with us, waiting to comfort us.

When you cry out today, take time to recognize that God is with you and allow Him to comfort you.

DAY 80

"We are God's handiwork, created in Christ Jesus to do good works, which God has prepared in advance for us to do."

Ephesians 2:10

Perhaps the season of life we are in right now is preparing us for something important that God has planned for us to do. Through our pain He is molding us and refining us so that we'll have what we need to carry out His plan for our lives. It's been said that God never wastes a hurt and it is highly possible that the pain we are experiencing now can and will be used for His glory in the future.

Take a moment today to think about the ways that God has refined you through your experience as a Hurting Mom.

DAY 81

"As for God, his way is perfect; the Lord's word is flawless; he shields all who take refuge in him."

Psalm 18:30

We want so desperately to be shielded from the pain and anxiety we are experiencing over our child. The Bible tells us that God will be our shield if we take refuge in Him. The important word there is IF. We have a choice as to whether or not we seek comfort and refuge in Him. We so often try to find peace by our own imperfect means, but God's way is perfect.

Open up your Bible today and take refuge in the flawless Word of God. Take refuge in Him and allow Him to comfort you.

DAY 82

"See what great love the great Father has lavished on us, that we should be called children of God! And that is what we are!"

1 John 3:1a

When we are hurting over our child we don't feel very loveable, do we? We feel tired, beaten down, and haggard. Everything around us seems dull and it is hard to accept that our Father, or anyone for that matter, could "lavish" love on us. But we are His children and because He loves us so much, He grieves over us in our pain just as we grieve over our children.

Allow God's love to permeate the dullness around you today and get hold of the idea that you are His child and He loves you.

DAY 83

"You shall rejoice in all the good things the Lord your God has given to you and your household."

Deuteronomy 26:11b

Rejoicing is the last thing we want to think about when we are grieving over the decisions of our child. We feel that there is nothing good in our lives and we will never be happy or have joy again. But if we are intentional about looking for the good things God has given us, we will be able to recognize the way that He has provided for us and we might even find some things to rejoice about.

Take some time today to look for some of the good things that God has given to you and thank Him.

DAY 84

"The Lord is not slow in keeping his promise, as some understand slowness. Instead he is patient with you, not wanting anyone to perish, but everyone to come to repentance."

2 Peter 3:9

Sometimes it seems that God is so slow to answer our prayers, doesn't it? But God deals in eternity, so what seems exceedingly slow to us is a blink of an eye to Him. The important thing to remember is that, just as He is patient and never gives up on us, we need to do the same when it comes to our child. Be patient, believing that God, who loves our children more than we do, is also patiently waiting for them to turn around.

Think about some of the times that God has answered your prayers and thank Him for His perfect timing.

DAY 85

"I waited patiently for the Lord; he turned to me and heard my cry. He lifted me out of the slimy pit, out of the mud and mire; he set my feet on a rock and gave me a firm place to stand."

Psalm 40:1-2

We get so caught up in our disappointment and pain over our child that we feel the God doesn't hear us. It seems like we are sinking into a pit and we don't see how there can possibly be a way out. This verse assures us that God does hear our cries and He will lift us up and help us to stand firm again.

Commit to being patient as you wait for the Lord to answer your prayers. Allow Him to pull you out of the mud and mire knowing that He loves you and is with you.

"For where two or three gather in my name, there am I with them."

Matthew 18:20

When we are suffering over our child we tend to isolate because we are ashamed, angry, and hurt. But, Jesus told us that there is something powerful that happens when we come together in His name. We were created to be in community and we need each other. Healing takes place when we talk about our troubles and as we listen to others.

Reach out to someone you trust today and share your burdens. Ask them to pray for you and your child and commit to praying for them.

DAY 87

"Even though I walk through the darkest valley, I will fear no evil, for you are with me; your rod and your staff, they comfort me."

Psalm 23:4

Let's face it; our deepest fear is that our child is going to die because of the way they are living. It's very difficult and painful to even think about that, but it is the unspoken reason for our anxiety and fear. In the 23rd Psalm we are assured that God is with us and He will comfort us.

Take some time today to sit quietly and be aware of God's presence with you, and then ask Him to comfort you in the way that only He can.

DAY 88

"Therefore do not worry about tomorrow, for tomorrow will worry about itself. Each day has enough trouble of its own."

Matthew 6:34

We spend so much time worrying about things that, for the most part, never happen, don't we? The "what ifs" threaten to consume us and it is hard to enjoy the good things that happen today because of our worry about what might happen tomorrow. Jesus tells us not to worry about tomorrow, in other words, live in the present. Put your focus and your energy on dealing with what is going on right now, instead of what could happen down the road.

Today, when you catch yourself beginning to worry about something that hasn't happened, surrender it to Jesus.

DAY 89

"In peace I will lie down and sleep, for you alone, Lord, make me dwell in safety."

Psalm 4:8b

As Hurting Moms we experience many sleepless nights. It's when things get quiet and we lay our head on our pillow that worry and anxiety take over. We ache over what is happening with our child and sleep alludes us. This Psalm reminds us that it is the Lord alone who will give us what we need to sleep in peace.

When you go to bed tonight, surrender all of your worry to God. Allow Him to give you the peace you so desperately need so that you can sleep.

DAY 90

"When you pass through the waters, I will be with you; and when you pass through the rivers, they will not sweep over you. When you walk through the fire, you will not be burned; the flames will not set you ablaze. For I am the Lord your God, the Holy One of Israel, your Savior." Isaiah 43:2-3a

We can relate to this Scripture because at one time or another all Hurting Moms feel as though we are being swept away with an unstoppable current one moment and that we are ablaze with fire the next. How comforting it is to remember that God is with us through it all. He is our protector, our savior, and will not let us be overcome with the painful things that threaten to control and consume us.

When the negative forces begin to close in on you, focus on your savior who is right there with you. Allow Him to protect you today.

DAY 91

"And my God will meet all your needs according to the riches of his glory in Christ Jesus."

Philippians 4:19

Our greatest need is to have a sense of peace and joy in our lives again. We need a break from the constant worry and the nagging ache in the pit of our stomach. We need rest! We are reminded in this verse that God will meet all of our needs. The problem is that we sometimes hold on so tightly to the very things that are hurting us that we miss out on the peace that God is patiently waiting to give to us.

Try to let go of the worry and fear you have today. Spend some time thinking about how God has demonstrated His amazing love for you and for your child by sending His Son, Jesus. Allow Him to meet your needs.

DAY 92

"When I said, 'My foot is slipping,'
your love, O Lord, supported me.
When anxiety was great within me,
your consolation brought me joy."

Psalm 94:18-19

We are so consumed with worry and anxiety that sometimes we feel as if we are slipping and that we are surely going to fall. But if we stop to remember that the Lord is with us and loves us, it will give us a firm foothold again and we are able to keep going. He is the one who can and will support us when everything appears to be caving in on us. It is even possible to have joy if we allow Him to console us.

Take some time to read your Bible today. Open yourself up to God's love, support, and consolation and experience relief from your anxiety.

DAY 93

"If any of you lacks wisdom, you should ask God, who gives generously to all without finding fault, and it will be given to you."

James 1:5

How many times do we wish we knew what to do or what to say in regards to our child? We don't know how to set boundaries and stick with it. We are confused about where our role as the mom ends and codependency and enabling takes over. We need WISDOM! In this verse we are told that God will generously give us wisdom if we ask Him for it. Best of all, He won't find fault with us. He knows we are doing the best we can and He wants to help us.

As you pray today, ask God specifically for wisdom, believing that He will generously give it to you without finding fault.

DAY 94

"God anointed us, set his seal of ownership on us, and put his Spirit in our hearts as a deposit, guaranteeing what is to come."

2 Corinthians 1:21b-22

One of the greatest sources of our fear is not knowing what is going to happen next with our child. It is so hard to move through our day when we feel like everything is out of our control. But God has given us His Spirit, we belong to Him and He will give us everything we need to face the challenges that may or may not be around the corner.

Trust God to give you what you need for anything the future may hold for you and your child. Get in touch with His Spirit, which is already in and around you, and let Him support and strengthen you.

DAY 95

"My God is my rock, in whom I take refuge, my shield and the horn of my salvation. He is my stronghold, my refuge and my savior."

2 Samuel 22:3a

We suffer in silence trying to make it through another day, putting up a good front, pasting on a fake smile, using nothing but our own strength. We feel so exposed and alone, but it doesn't have to be that way! We can take refuge in the God who loves us and our child. It is our choice to allow Him to shield and save us from our anguish or to hold onto it and continue trying to get through our days on our own.

Make the choice to let God be your stronghold today. Allow Him to shield you as you take refuge in Him.

DAY 96

"The Spirit helps us in our weakness. For we do not know what to pray for as we ought, but the Spirit himself intercedes for us with groanings too deep for words."

Romans 8:26b (ESV)

Sometimes our pain is so great and we feel so weak and helpless that we have no idea how we should pray. When we find it impossible to express ourselves to God, we can allow the Holy Spirit to intercede for us. Remember, God already knows exactly what we are feeling and it isn't always necessary for us to "talk" to Him. The important thing is that we "be" with Him, simply experiencing His presence.

Spend some time sitting quietly with God today. Allow His Spirit to surround you as you rest in the knowledge that He is the one who can and will comfort you even if you don't have words to express yourself.

DAY 97

"The Lord will fight for you;
you need only to be still."

Exodus 14:14

We feel like we are in a battle and it is exhausting! We are fighting to fix, control, and save our child. We are fighting against the guilt and shame we have because of his or her actions. We are fighting to maintain our sanity because we are anxious and fearful every hour of the day. This verse is such a great reminder that what we really need to do is be still. The Lord is in this with us and He knows what needs to be done. He will fight for us if we will just "be still" and surrender it all to Him.

Make a conscious choice to turn over your battles to the Lord today. Be still and know that He is with you and He is in control.

DAY 98

"May the Lord direct your hearts into God's love and Christ's perseverance."

2 Thessalonians 3:5

We are stressed and tired because we are working so hard to control a situation that is totally out of our control. We have started to lose sight of who we are in Christ and forgotten how much we are loved by Him. This verse reminds us to refocus our heart toward God's love. It also assures us that we can rest in the knowledge that Christ is hanging in there for us and He will not give up on our child or on us. He is faithful.

Turn toward God today, focusing your heart on His love and faithfulness.

DAY 99

"The Lord gives strength to his people; the Lord blesses his people with peace."

Psalm 29:11

The only place we are going to receive strength to carry on is from the Lord. We will not find the strength we are seeking by taking more vitamins, working out, or stuffing down our feelings of pain. It is the Lord who will give us strength to face whatever is coming our way next. When we trust Him to give us strength we will also be blessed with His perfect peace.

Make the choice to trust God for strength and peace today.

DAY 100

"Be joyful in hope, patient in affliction, faithful in prayer."

Romans 12:12

It seems that the situation with our child and the pain we are experiencing has been going on forever, and as time passes we begin to lose hope. Without hope, there is no joy. We are tired of losing sleep and of having a perpetual knot in the pit of our stomach. We have been patient long enough! However, the Bible tells us to be patient in our pain and to continue to pray faithfully. Our hope is in the Lord, not in what our child is doing or not doing. It is time to redirect our attention to God so that we can once again experience hope and joy.

Spend some time in prayer today asking God for continued patience and the hope that comes only from Him.

DAY 101

"The Lord is good, a refuge in times of trouble. He cares for those who trust in him."

Nahum 1:7

When we have a child who is out of control we are definitely experiencing a time of trouble. We lose sight of anything good and our focus is fixed on the child who is hurting us. But the Lord is good and He can give us relief from the pain. He cares about us and He wants us to trust Him.

Think about the good things in your life today and make a conscious decision to trust God to be your refuge from the negative and painful things you are experiencing.

DAY 102

"How gracious God will be when you cry for help! As soon as he hears, he will answer you."

Isaiah 30:19b

We can be assured that God does hear our prayers and has compassion for us. We are promised in this verse that God is gracious to us when we cry for help. That means He is kind to us in our time of need. He is in the process of answering us right now, even if we can't see anything happening yet.

In what ways have you experienced God's grace in your life? How can remembering how He has been gracious to you in the past encourage you today?

DAY 103

"This I call to mind and therefore I have hope: Because of the Lord's great love we are not consumed, for his compassions never fail."

Lamentations 3:21-22

On those days when we feel consumed with grief we can remember, or "call to mind" the love of God, reminding ourselves of His compassion for us. It's amazing how quickly we begin to experience a lessening of our pain when we realize that we are not alone. Through God's love and the compassion He has for us, we can sense His comforting presence with us.

Call to mind God's great love and compassion for you. Allow these things to give you hope.

DAY 104

"The Lord is good to those whose hope is in him, to the one who seeks him."

Lamentations 3:25

Are you putting your hope in your child? Is your total sense of wellbeing wrapped up in what he or she is doing or not doing? Do you feel like you will not be able to experience joy until they turn around? This verse tells us that our hope should be in the Lord. We can begin to experience that hope if we actively seek Him. That means we are praying, reading our Bible, spending time in fellowship with other followers of Christ, spending time in nature, doing the things that help us feel closer to God.

Spend some time doing something that makes you feel closer to God today.

DAY 105

"You have allowed me to suffer much hardship, but you will restore me to life again and lift me up from the depths of the earth. You will restore me to even greater honor and comfort me once again."
Psalm 71:20-21(NLT)

The psalmist writes with such confidence! He is not asking for a restored life, honor or comfort, but rather he is boldly declaring the things he knows that God is going to do. Sometimes it feels like we are asking for the same things over and over again and we wonder if He hears us. How confident are you that God will comfort you, heal your pain, and restore you to life again?

Think about some times in your life that God has answered your prayers and then go to Him in confidence with your request for comfort and restoration.

"Shout for joy, you heavens; rejoice, you earth; burst into song, you mountains! For the Lord comforts his people and will have compassion on his afflicted ones."

Isaiah 49:13

It's been awhile since we have felt like rejoicing! We keep hearing that God is compassionate and wants to comfort us, but we are still overwhelmed with anxiety, grief, and sadness. Could it be that we are not open to the comfort God wants to give us? Do we hold on too tightly to our pain so that we cannot sense His compassion? Sometimes we have to "fake it until we make it". We all have things to be grateful for or even to rejoice about, but the heaviness in our heart prevents us from shouting for joy about anything.

Find one thing that you can rejoice about today and shout for joy!

DAY 107

"May your unfailing love be my comfort according to your promise to your servant."

Psalm 119:76

How are you serving the Lord these days? We get so caught up in focusing on our child that we forget about our own relationship with our Father. Somewhere along the line we stop using the gifts He has given us and we forget about the things we used to be passionate about because we are so caught up in our grief and pain. God has promised us that His love for us is unfailing. We can definitely find comfort in that alone, but if we are serving Him and others, even in the midst of our suffering, we will experience a deeper level of wellbeing.

Find a way to serve someone else today and pay attention to the relief and sense of wellbeing that you feel.

DAY 108

"For I can do everything through Christ who gives me strength."

Philippians 4:13 (NLT)

When we are tapped out and our strength and courage are basically non-existent we need to remember this verse. This verse, from Paul's letter to the people at Philippi, expresses the surety that God will give us the strength to carry on. He will give us what we need to take care of the rest of our family when we feel as though we can't put one foot in front of the other and we have a hard time maintaining a logical thought pattern. He will also give us the strength to set healthy boundaries with our child and stick with them. It's no wonder we feel we can't make it through another day when we are relying on our own strength instead of God's strength.

Ask God for strength today and open yourself up to receiving it. Allow Him to carry your burdens of anxiety, fear, and grief so that you will be able to start and complete the tasks that are before you.

DAY 109

". . . being confident of this, that he who began a good work in you will carry it on to completion until the day of Christ Jesus."

Philippians 1:6

Oh what a relief it is to know that God is not finished with us or our kids yet! Take comfort in knowing that even though you might not be able to see it right now, He is working in you, using this difficult time in your life to mold you into the woman He created you to be. At the same time He is working, always working, in our children. He loves them more than we do and He created them with a purpose. Our job during this time is to stand in the gap in prayer for our kids.

Stand in the gap in prayer for your child today. Ask God to keep them safe and to bring people along their path that will point the way to Him. While you are at it – pray for peace for yourself! God is faithful and He will answer your prayers.

DAY 110

"When I called, you answered me; you made me bold and stouthearted."

Psalm 138:3

Some synonyms for stouthearted are brave, determined, courageous and stubborn. These are things that we, as Hurting Moms, need in order to deal with our child and everything else we have going on in our lives. We want to be brave and courageous as we face whatever is going to happen next. Determination is what will help us overcome the feelings of helplessness that we are experiencing. And when it comes to protecting ourselves and others in our family, we need to set boundaries and then be stubborn about sticking to them. This Psalm tells us that when we call on God and ask Him for these things He will answer us.

Call out to God today and ask Him for the things that are going to help you deal with all you have going on today.

DAY 111

"Do not fear, for I have redeemed you; I have summoned you by name; you are mine. When you pass through the waters, I will be with you; and when you pass through the rivers, they will not sweep over you. When you walk through the fire, you will not be burned; the flames will not set you ablaze. For I am the Lord your God, the Holy One of Israel, your Savior."
Isaiah 43:1b-3a

We are in such turmoil and our emotions change from moment to moment so that we sometimes feel like we are being swept down a river or that we are walking through a fire. One moment we feel compassion for our child, the next moment we are angry, and the next moment we are so brokenhearted that all we can do is cry. It's comforting to know that God knows us by name and claims us as His own. We may feel totally alone, but we are not alone because He has promised us that He is with us through it all and He is our Savior.

God is right there with you no matter which emotions you are feeling today. Talk to Him and express what you are feeling as you allow Him to comfort and protect you.

DAY 112

"In him and through faith in him we may approach God with freedom and confidence."

Ephesians 3:12

Through our faith in Jesus Christ we have the freedom to talk to God with confidence that He hears us. Jesus bridged the gap between us and God when He died on the cross to pay the price for our sin. When we accept what Jesus did for us on the cross and believe that He rose from the dead, we step out in faith to follow Him. Once we have made the decision to do that we can be confident that God not only hears us, but He answers our prayers.

If you haven't made the choice to follow Jesus, do it today. Surrender yourself (and your child) to Him and allow Him to start working in your life to give you peace and joy, no matter what else is going on.

DAY 113

"So do not throw away your confidence; it will be richly rewarded. You need to persevere so that when you have done the will of God, you will receive what he has promised."

Hebrews 10:35-36

It's hard to be confident when day after day, week after week, sometimes year after year, our child continues to make choices that keep them on a path of destruction. We are so focused on them that we completely lose sight of God's will for our own lives. Everything just seems to stand still for us. God wants us to persevere in seeking His will for our own lives, even during this difficult time. As we put God first we stay strong and confident in Him and we are richly rewarded by things like a good night sleep, a sense of wellbeing and the peace that we are seeking.

Spend some time today regrouping and seeking God's will for your life.

DAY 114

"Let the morning bring me word of your unfailing love, for I have put my trust in you. Show me the way I should go, for to you I entrust my life."

Psalm 143:8

Everything seems a little better in the morning, doesn't it? As we lay awake churning in the night, our pain seems almost unbearable. But when the morning comes it doesn't seem quite as huge and we are relieved to have made it through the night. In the morning we can once again put our trust in our God and remember that He loves us with unfailing love.

When the morning comes, seek promises of God's unfailing love in His Word and entrust your life and the life of your child to Him.

DAY 115

"So I say to you: Ask and it will be given to you; seek and you will find; knock and the door will be opened to you. For everyone who asks receives; the one who seeks finds; and to the one who knocks, the door will be opened."

Luke 11:9

These words of Jesus remind us that He is waiting for us to seek Him so that He can answer our prayers. So many times we ask, even beg, for Him to change our child and we overlook what He wants to do in our lives. We are so preoccupied with what our child is doing or not doing and we are so consumed with worry about them that we miss out on what God might be trying to teach us.

Spend time today seeking God with all your heart and be aware of the doors that begin to open through Him. They may not be directly related to your child, but they will definitely strengthen and encourage you. We just have to take our eyes off of our child long enough to discover what God has for us.

DAY 116

"Teach me knowledge and good judgment, for I trust your commands."

Psalm 119:66

Oh how we long for someone to tell us what to do. How do we handle this child? How do we handle the pain we are in? How do we find time or energy to pay attention to the rest of our family? How can we make it through one more day? The answer to all of these questions is to trust God. Trust Him to give you the knowledge and good judgment to make the right decisions. Slow down long enough to spend time in His Word and to talk to Him. Most importantly, be still and listen to Him.

Spend some time sitting quietly and "listening" to God today. You may hear Him in the form of a thought, or by being led to a significant scripture in your Bible. Ask Him to give you knowledge and good judgment as you process any decision you are in the midst of making.

DAY 117

"For this God is our God for ever and ever; he will be our guide even to the end."

Psalm 48:14

Our relationship with our God is a very personal thing. We are special in His eyes and He will continue to be our God forever – no matter what happens while we are here on Earth. He loves us so much that He wants to guide us for our whole lives. Whether we are going through good times or bad, He will guide us by way of His Holy Spirit if we will allow Him to. That's a really big IF! It is up to us to open ourselves up to His guidance.

Set aside your own agenda today and allow God to be your guide.

DAY 118

"And this is my prayer: that your love may abound more and more in knowledge and depth of insight, so that you may be able to discern what is best and may be pure and blameless for the day of Christ, filled with the fruit of righteousness that comes through Jesus Christ – to the glory and praise of God."

Philippians 1:9-11

That's what we need, isn't it? Every day as we deal with our child we wish we had more knowledge, insight, and discernment. We love our child so much, but we feel so ill-equipped to know how to handle them. Are they telling us the truth? We want to believe them, but we don't always have the insight or discernment to know what is true or when we are being manipulated. When we surrender our child along with our anxiety about how to deal with them to Jesus, we will receive not only a sense of peace, but He will help us to gain the insight we are looking for.

Surrender your child to Jesus today, praying for knowledge, insight and discernment as you make decisions on how to deal with them.

DAY 119

"But God demonstrates his own love for us in this: While we were still sinners, Christ died for us."

Romans 5:8

It's not just that Christ loves us. He loves our kids too. This means that no matter what our children are doing or not doing, Christ died for them, just like He died for us, because He loves them so much. Sometimes when we are having a hard time feeling love for our child, it's nice to know that Christ loves them in spite of what they are doing.

Take comfort today knowing that even if you are feeling angry or indifferent to your child, Christ is loving them more than they can comprehend. Enjoy His perfect peace as you surrender your burden to Him.

"Whatever happens conduct yourselves in a manner worthy of the gospel of Christ."

Philippians 1:27a

That's a lot easier said than done, isn't it? The frustration, discouragement and anguish that we feel over the situation with our child often causes our actions to be anything but worthy of the gospel of Christ. The way we think, talk, and act has a lot to do with how much time we are spending with the Lord. On our own we are powerless to conduct ourselves in a manner worthy of Christ. But when we allow Him to work in and through us we are able to overcome our bad attitudes so that we can reflect His love in the way we conduct ourselves.

Allow Jesus to be the one to influence your thoughts and actions today.

DAY 121

"Surely God is my salvation; I will trust and not be afraid. The Lord, the Lord himself, is my strength and my defense; he has become my salvation."

Isaiah 12:2

How many times do we surrender our child to God, but then take back the burdens of worry and fear? Trusting God has to be a moment by moment, day by day decision. Our child is not the only one who needs salvation right now. We are in great need of salvation as well. We need salvation from our anxiety, our anger, our guilt and our shame.

Read this verse throughout the day today. Engrain this truth that God is your strength, your joy, your peace, and your salvation into your heart and surrender your burdens to Him.

DAY 122

"Commit to the Lord whatever you do, and he will establish your plans."

Proverbs 16:3

Before you have that family meeting or hard conversation, before you make any decision regarding your interaction with your child, pray and seek God's guidance. We so often fly off the handle in a moment of anger or in the midst of our pain. Those plans that we make on our own without inviting God to be part of it don't usually work out too well.

Today be sure to commit to God any plan that you make or any hard conversation that you must have. Allow Him to guide and direct you.

DAY 123

"Some people make cutting remarks, but the words of the wise bring healing."

Proverbs 12:18 (NLT)

How many times have we spewed out words that we wish we could take back? How often has it been our angry words to our child, spoken out of frustration and hurt, that drives an even bigger wedge between us and them? This Proverb reminds us that if we think before we speak, before we lash out with something mean or hurtful, it can be a step closer to healing our relationships instead of three steps backwards.

Ask God to give you wisdom when you communicate with your child so that your words can lead to healing for both of you.

DAY 124

*"Humble yourselves before the Lord,
and he will lift you up."*
James 4:10

The situation we are in with our child causes us to be ashamed. We don't like to talk about what we are experiencing with other people and we cringe when we hear our friends and family talk about their "perfect" kids. For the most part, we suffer in silence and alone. To protect ourselves we tend to isolate and harden ourselves before others and even before God. When we go before God and humble ourselves, crying out, confessing our own sin, and opening ourselves up to His care and control, we will experience relief from our shame and our pain.

Go to God today. Repent of your own sin and re-surrender yourself and your child to Him. Allow Him to be in control today and you will be lifted up.

DAY 125

"He will cover you with his feathers, and under his wings you will find refuge; his faithfulness will be your shield and rampart."

Psalm 91:4

The dictionary defines rampart as a protective barrier. Oh, how we long for a barrier to protect us from the agonizing emotions we have because of the choices our child is making. How comforting it is to know that in God we can find a safe refuge. He will shield us and be our rampart from the heartache. He is always faithful and we can count on Him to shield and protect us.

Take refuge in God and allow Him to be your rampart today.

DAY 126

"You are my hiding place; you will protect me from trouble and surround me with songs of deliverance."

Psalm 32:7

We try to hide by isolating, or going out with fake smiles plastered on our faces. Our hearts are breaking into a million pieces and all we want to do is run away from the pain we are in. We are beginning to realize that we cannot protect our child from the choices they are making, but how can we protect ourselves from the anguish we are experiencing? This Psalm tells us that God alone is our hiding place and He will protect us. If we seek Him we will begin to have the peace for which we are longing.

Give your burden to the Lord. Allow Him to protect you from the fear, anxiety and hurt you are feeling. Once you have surrendered it all to Him, listen for the songs of deliverance, and enjoy the freedom He will give you.

DAY 127

"Consider it pure joy, my brothers and sisters, whenever you face trials of many kinds, because you know that the testing of your faith produces perseverance. Let perseverance finish its work so that you may be mature and complete, not lacking anything."

James 1:2-4

Joy is the furthest thing from our hearts and minds when we are in the midst of our struggle as a Hurting Mom. However, James says when our faith is tested we develop perseverance, or the quality that allows us to continue to move forward, even in difficult times. Although we feel paralyzed with fear and anxiety, we must continue to rely on God to give us what we need to get through each day. And as we learn to trust Him, we will mature in our faith so that we can experience the joy and peace that we desire.

Ask God to help you persevere and then trust Him to give you everything you need to make it through this day.

DAY 128

"Therefore, if anyone is in Christ, the new creation has come. The old has gone, the new has here!"

2 Corinthians 5:17

We experience a lot of guilt and shame when we have a child that is out of control. We feel like we are a failure as a parent and we keep going back over the past looking for the things that we have done wrong to cause this to happen. We are ashamed because we feel that everyone else has a perfect kid and they must be judging us. This verse reminds us that when we surrender our lives to Jesus and commit to following Him we become a new creation. We no longer have to identify with the mistakes we may have made or what happened in the past. We can take delight in finding our new identity in Him instead of in the way we think others may or may not perceive us.

Spend time identifying the ways in which you are a new creation in Christ.

DAY 129

"Stand firm. Let nothing move you. Always give yourselves fully to the work of the Lord, because you know that your labor in the Lord is not in vain."

1 Corinthians 15:58b

We labor over our kids, don't we? We try anything and everything to try to gain control over what is happening with them, but for the most part our efforts are in vain. When we labor in the Lord, in other words, we put our energy and our focus on serving the Lord; we are not laboring in vain. The more fully we give ourselves to the things He want us to do, using the gifts He has given us, the stronger we will be. We will be able to stand firm in Him no matter what this day brings.

Find a way to serve the Lord by serving someone else today and see how much better you will feel.

DAY 130

"Have faith in the Lord your God and you will be upheld."
2 Chronicles 20:20b

When you grow tired of making every decision by yourself and trying to fix or control your child in vain, put your faith in the God who created and loves you. He has a plan for your life and for the life of your child and He wants to have a relationship with you. When you stop fighting to do it all on your own power He will uphold you, just as He has promised to do.

Make an intentional decision to stop relying on yourself and put your faith in God today in order to experience relief from the struggle.

DAY 131

"For God has not despised or scorned the suffering of the afflicted one; he has not hidden his face from him but has listened to his cry for help."

Psalm 22:24

Because of the guilt and the shame associated with being a Hurting Mom we often feel that we are not worthy to cry out to the Lord for help. We are afraid that He does not care about our suffering because to some degree we feel that we have brought this on ourselves. But this verse assures us that He does listen to our cries for help. He will not hide from us, but rather He welcomes us to turn to Him for wisdom and comfort.

Allow God to comfort you today remembering that He loves you and is waiting for you to trust Him.

DAY 132

"This is the confidence we have in approaching God: that if we ask anything according to his will, he hears us."

1 John 5:14

It is God's will that we believe in Him and trust in Him, just as that is also His will for our children. We can and should approach the Lord with confidence when we are asking for the salvation of our kids, and we are assured that He does hear us. We can come to our Father with any request and know that if it is within His will, He will hear us and answer accordingly. That doesn't always mean that our specific prayers are answered immediately the way we think they should be answered. But it does mean that we should be bold when we pray, knowing that God hears us and is working in ways that we can't understand.

Approach God with confidence today as you pray for your child. He hears you!

DAY 133

"Come with me by yourselves to a quiet pace and get some rest."

Mark 6:31b

These are the words of Jesus to His apostles when they were being pulled in many directions. We often feel that way don't we? We are exhausted with worry and anxiety over our wayward child, and then there are all of the other demands that are on us. We have jobs to go to, other kids who need our attention, a house to clean, bills to pay, church and school activities, etc., etc. Jesus reminds us that true rest and peace will come when we get away to a quiet place and spend time alone with Him.

Put aside the distractions in your life for awhile and spend some time alone with Jesus today.

"Show me your ways; Lord, teach me your paths. Guide me in your truth and teach me; for you are God my Savior, and my hope is in you all day long."

Psalm 25:4-5

DAY 134

God will use the pain we are experiencing if we will open ourselves up and allow Him to teach us. He has a plan and a path for us, even in the midst of the struggle, but we have to be willing to be guided by Him. Our hope is not found in what our child is doing or not doing, it is found in Jesus.

Let go of all of your own plans and surrender to God's plan. Put your hope in Him today and seek the path He has for you.

DAY 135

"It is for freedom that Christ has set us free. Stand firm, then, and do not let yourselves be burdened again by a yoke of slavery."

Galatians 5:1

The hurt we have over our child really is like a yoke of slavery, isn't it? We feel so weighted down with our anxiety and pain that is sometimes difficult to stand at all. This verse reminds us that in Christ we can find freedom from all of the negative emotions we are feeling. He can and will lift our burdens when we turn to Him.

Stand up straight, throw your shoulders back, hold your head up and give your burdens to Jesus today. Allow Him to calm you and comfort you. Find your confidence in Him today.

"I keep asking that the God of our Lord Jesus Christ, the glorious Father, may give you the Spirit of wisdom and revelation, so that you many know him better."

Ephesians 1:17

DAY 136

We may ask God for wisdom and revelation in order to know how to deal with our children. We are always looking for new ways to reel them in, control them, and get them on a different path than the one they are on. But this verse is very clear that the things for which we ask should be for the purpose of knowing God better. We don't really have any control over our kids, but as we seek to grow deeper in our relationship with our loving Father, we will begin to have the peace and joy in our lives that we long for.

Ask God for wisdom and revelation in order to know Him better today.

DAY 137

But Jesus immediately said to them: "Take courage! It is I. Don't be afraid."

Matthew 14:27

Jesus said these words to His disciples when he was walking on water toward them. They were terrified, thinking they were seeing a ghost, but He calmed their fears with these words. We know what it is to be terrified, don't we? We are terrified for the lives of our children.

Meditate on these powerful words of Jesus today when you feel fear taking over. Allow Him to comfort you, knowing He is with you and with your child. If He can walk on water, surely He can heal us and protect our children.

DAY 138

"Let us therefore make every effort to do what leads to peace and to mutual edification."

Romans 14:19

What will lead to peace and mutual edification? We know what peace is and to edify is to elevate, enrich, lift, better, improve, or transform. We want those things, don't we? However, we won't enjoy a sense of peace and we won't be edified if we continue to be consumed by the child who is out of our control.

Start today to direct your efforts and energy toward obtaining the peace and edification that this verse talks about. You can start by opening up your Bible and seeking the promises of God.

DAY 139

"May these words of my mouth and this meditation of my heart be pleasing in your sight, Lord, my Rock and my Redeemer."

Psalm 19:14

In the midst of our frustrations and hurt we have feelings of bitterness, resentment, fear, and angst in our heart and sometimes that painful stuff manifests itself in the words that come out of our mouth. These negative emotions are not of God and they are definitely not pleasing in His sight. He is the one who gives us strength and redeems us, but it is hard to seek Him when we are dwelling on the things that are tearing us down.

Examine your heart today. Are your thoughts and the things you are holding onto pleasing to God? Ask Him to give you the strength and the discipline to check your words before they come out of your mouth.

DAY 140

"Let us hold unswervingly to the hope we profess for he who promised is faithful."

Hebrews 10:23

The hope in this verse is Jesus Christ. He has promised that if we surrender everything to Him and walk in His light we will have not only eternal life with Him in Heaven, but we can have a rich, full life with Him here on earth as well. As we follow Him and seek His will for our lives, He is faithful to provide us with peace and joy. Our hope is in Him, not in what our child is doing or not doing.

Shift your hope away from what your child may or may not do today. Put your hope and your focus on the Lord who has you both in the palm of His hand.

DAY 141

"Yes, my soul, find rest in God; my hope comes from him. Truly he is my rock and may salvation; he is my fortress, I will not be shaken."

Psalm 62:5,6

It's true; we cannot not find rest apart from God. He is our hope and He will fortify us and give us what we need to overcome the constant battle with the fear and anxiety that threaten to overcome us. If we battle alone, we have no hope of finding freedom.   But if we place our hope in the Lord, by turning to Him for guidance, strength and courage, we will realize the peace and rest we have been seeking.

Surrender your battles to the Lord today and allow Him to give you rest.

DAY 142

"Now to him who is able to do immeasurable more than all we ask or imagine, according to his power that is at work within us, to him be glory in the church and in Christ Jesus throughout all generations, for ever and ever!"

Ephesians 3:20-21

It seems like nothing is changing. Our child is not turning around and we are exhausted and feeling hopeless. This verse reminds us that God is able to do everything we ask and more. We get discouraged because we can't see anything happening, but God has a plan that is bigger and better than we can imagine. And His power is at work within us and in our child right now. We sometimes get in the way of what He is doing because we get impatient and try to control the situation in our own way.

Re-surrender yourself and your child to the God who is able to do more than that you have asked for or can even imagine. Trust Him with everything today.

DAY 143

"Ask and it will be given to you; seek and you will find; knock and the door will be opened to you. For everyone who asks receives; the one who seeks finds; and to the one who knocks; the door will be opened."

Matthew 7:7-8

God loves us and wants us to have joy and peace in our lives. More than anything He wants to have a relationship with us. The problem is that our relationship with Him often revolves around our requests, but we don't really spend time seeking Him. If asking for things is the basis for our connection with God, we will miss out on the relationship that He wants to have with us. It is only through a loving, trusting relationship with Him that we will experience the peace and sense of wellbeing that we are looking for.

Spend some time truly seeking the Lord today.

DAY 144

"For the eyes of the Lord range throughout the earth to strengthen those whose hearts are fully committed to him."

2 Chronicles 16:9a

God is looking for us to be fully committed to Him. Once we have committed ourselves to Him, above anything else, we will be strengthened. We want God to help us, but so often we put other things in front of our commitment to Him. We cannot be fully committed to God when we are allowing other things to distract us.

What are some of the things that you are putting before God today? Surrender those things to Him and recommit your life to Him. Fully commit to Him by placing Him above all else.

DAY 145

"We know that God does not listen to sinners. He listens to the godly person who does his will."

John 9:31

We have begged God to bring our child back but it seems that He is not listening to us. Perhaps we have things in our own lives that need to be addressed. Are we seeking a deeper personal relationship with God and being obedient in doing His will? Perhaps it's time for us to think about the ways we can go deeper in our relationship with Him instead of focusing on trying to fix and control our child.

Spend time alone with God today, not only to ask Him for things on behalf of your child, but to seek His will in your own life.

DAY 146

"Let us draw near to God with a sincere heart and with the full assurance that faith brings, having our hearts sprinkled to cleanse us from a guilty conscience and having our bodies washed with pure water."

Hebrews 10:22

We carry a lot of guilt and shame because of what is happening with our child. We blame ourselves and we feel unworthy to approach God with our requests for ourselves or for our kids. But by trusting God and placing our faith in Him, we can draw near to Him with confidence that He hears our prayers. We are His children and He wants to cleanse our heart from the painful burdens that we bear.

Recommit to placing your faith in the God who loves you today, and then draw near to Him for relief from your guilt and pain.

DAY 147

"We confidently and joyfully look forward to sharing God's glory. So now we can rejoice in our wonderful new relationship with God because our Lord Jesus Christ has made us friends of God."

Romans 5:2b,11b (NLT)

We don't feel like we have anything to rejoice about. How can we possibly rejoice when our child is out of control and every waking moment is filled with worry, anxiety, and pain? We feel hopeless. This verse tells us that our hope is in the glory of God. If we put our focus on Him and on a closer relationship with Jesus Christ we will be able to experience joy again. We are not rejoicing about what is going on with our child, but we are rejoicing in the hope we have through Jesus.

Make a conscious decision to put your hope in Jesus today and rejoice in the fact that you can have a relationship with Him.

"Know therefore that the Lord your God is God; He is the faithful God, keeping his covenant of love to a thousand generations of those who love him and keep his commands."

Deuteronomy 7:9

DAY 148

When we continue to try to rescue, fix and control our children we get in the way of what God is trying to do in their lives. This verse tells us that He has a covenant of love for "thousands of generations". His love doesn't stop with us. It carries on to our children and their children and grandchildren. If anyone can turn them around it is Him. Our job is to love Him and keep His commands in our own lives as we allow Him to protect and teach our kids.

Thank God for His faithfulness today. Surrender your child to Him and then get out of the way so He can work in their lives.

DAY 149

"O Lord, you are so good, so ready to forgive, so full of unfailing love for all who ask for your help."

Psalm 86:5 (NLT)

Sometimes we are bound up with guilt and shame because we feel responsible for what is going on with our child. We know that there is a good chance that some of the choices we have made along the way have played a part and we don't feel worthy to approach God. We are reminded in this verse that God is forgiving, good and abounding in love. Don't be afraid to call to Him. He is waiting for you with open arms and in His love and forgiveness you will find comfort.

Call out to God today and accept His forgiveness and love.

DAY 150

"Not by might nor by power, but by my Spirit", says the Lord of Almighty.

Zechariah 4:6b

How often we try to control our kids by our own will or by using our own power. How has that worked out for you? Probably not well at all. It is only through the power of God that our children are going to turn around and it is only through His Spirit that we are going to find comfort, rest, and healing for our tired and broken hearts.

Stop fighting by using your own strength and tap into the Holy Spirit today, allowing Him to guide and direct you as you deal with your child. Open yourself up and receive the comfort and peace that only He can give you.

DAY 151

"Praise the Lord, my soul, and forget not all his benefits – who forgives all your sins and heals all your diseases, who redeems your life from the pit and crowns you with love and compassion."

Psalm 103 2-4

It's easy to forget about the benefits of having a relationship with the God who loves us and loves our children. We get so focused on our child that our relationships with others and even with God become secondary. But it is our loving Father who can heal us of the pain we are in and He alone can and will redeem our lives with love and compassion. It is in Him that we will find relief.

Take your focus off of your child for a while today and spend time with the One who can make a difference. Experience the love and compassion He has for you.

"Whatever you have learned or received or heard from me, or seen in me – put it into practice. And the God of peace will be with you."

Philippians 4:9

Paul is instructing the people of Philippi to follow His example of rejoicing in the Lord in all circumstances. When we praise God for His goodness and His grace, even in the midst of our struggles, we will receive the peace that we seek. It's not always easy, but we can all find at least one or two things in our lives to rejoice about.

Spend time praising the God who created and loves you. Allow His perfect peace to flow through and saturate you today.

DAY 153

"Moses answered the people, "Do not be afraid. Stand firm and you will see the deliverance the Lord will bring you today."

Exodus 14:13a

These were the words of Moses to the Israelites when they were terrified that they were going to die in the desert. Their emotions were out of control and they were literally crumbling before his eyes. Isn't that the way we feel in the face of what is happening with our children? Terrified, out of control, and falling apart? Our peace does not have to be dependent on what our child is doing but it is dependent on whether or not we allow God to deliver us by standing firm in our faith in Him.

Stand firm today, believing that God will deliver you from your fear and anxiety.

DAY 154

"May the God who gives endurance and the encouragement give you a spirit of unity among yourselves as you follow Christ Jesus, so that with one heart and mouth you may glorify the God and Father of our Lord Jesus Christ."

Romans 15:5-6

Do you know other moms who are hurting over their kids? As you follow Jesus, receiving the endurance and encouragement from Him that you need to get through each day, don't be afraid to reach out to other moms who might be going through similar struggles with their children. Your common pain will draw you together and give you a spirit of unity that will give you a whole new level of comfort and strength. There is something very powerful about moms praying together for their kids and each other.

Reach out to someone else today. Share your story and listen to theirs and then pray for them.

DAY 155

"But the Lord stood at my side and gave me strength, so that through me the message might be fully proclaimed and all the Gentiles might hear it."

2 Timothy 4:17a

Through our experience with pain and heartache, God can and will teach us about Himself, if we pay attention. We may not always recognize Him, but the Lord is always by our side and He wants to give us strength, comfort, and peace. The beautiful thing is that once we have received these things from Him, we can be the ones to offer hope to other moms who are going through the same things by sharing the message of what He has done in our lives.

Watch for opportunities to share your story with someone else today. Tell them about what God is doing or has done in your life.

DAY 156

"A bruised reed he will not break, and a smoldering wick he will not snuff out. In faithfulness he will bring forth justice; he will not falter or be discouraged till he establishes justice on earth. In his law the islands will put their hope."

Isaiah 42:3,4

In The Message this verse reads like this: "He won't brush aside the bruised and the hurt and he won't disregard the small and insignificant, but He'll steadily and firmly set things right. He won't tire out and He won't quit. He won't be stopped until He's finished his work – to set things right on earth."

WOW! What a beautiful promise. We are bruised and hurt and so are our kids, but this verse tells us that God is totally aware of everything that is going on and He will not disregard us. Even if we can't see it, He is steadily working to make things right. We may get tired, but God doesn't.

Hand your worry and anxiety over to the God who loves you and your child today. Place your confidence in your loving Father who continues to work behind the scenes while you rest.

DAY 157

"Do not let any unwholesome talk come out of your mouths, but only what is helpful for building others up according to their needs, that it may benefit those who listen."

Ephesians 4:29

In the midst of our pain we often lash out with anger. It is in those moments, when we allow our frustration to take over, that we tend to say things that we regret. It is somehow much easier to speak to the child who is hurting us in a way that is not helpful in building them up and doesn't in any way benefit them or anyone else who can hear us.

Be aware of how you are talking to and about your child today. Try to find one thing that you can say to them that might build them up.

"So then, just as you received Christ Jesus as Lord, continue to live your lives in him, rooted and built up in him, strengthened in the faith as you were taught, and overflowing with thankfulness."

Colossians 2:6,7

DAY 158

When we root ourselves in anything other than Jesus we miss out on so much. He is the one who will build us up and strengthen us as we face the challenges in our lives. And what we are going through with our child is definitely a challenge. When we shift our focus off of the negative and painful things associated with our child and we keep our eyes on the Lord we can begin to see the things for which we are grateful and our hearts overflow with thanksgiving.

Think about the things you are thankful for today. Write them down, thank God, and pay attention to how much better you will feel.

DAY 159

"Set your minds on things above, not on earthly things."

Colossians 3:2

The situation with our child, the pain and heartache that we feel, along with the anxiety and fear, are earthly things. It's hard not to allow them to fill our minds and our very souls during every waking moment. But this Scripture tells us to set our minds on things above, positive things, things that are of God.

When you find yourself drowning in negative and painful emotions today, make a conscious decision to turn away from them and set your mind on Christ and the good things that He has for you.

"This is what the Sovereign Lord, the Holy One of Israel says: 'In repentance and rest is your salvation, in quietness and trust is your strength.'"

Isaiah 30:15a

Some of the pain we are experiencing is due to the guilt that we have when our child in out of control. We are so focused on them that we forget to spend time looking at our own lives and paying attention to the areas in which we need to repent. God loves us just as we love our children and He will give us rest and strength if we will just be quiet, repent for our own sin, and then trust in Him.

Slow down and spend some quality time with the Lord today. Trust Him to handle things for you and then rest, knowing that He is in control.

DAY 161

"But I trust in your unfailing love;
my heart rejoices in your salvation.
I will sing to the Lord's praise,
for he has been good to me."

Psalm 13:5-6

Trusting, rejoicing and singing are all things we can do to experience relief from our heartache. We can make a conscious decision, or choose, to trust God. And then we can rejoice in the fact that He loves our children just as He loves us. Because of His great love we have been saved and we can take comfort in knowing that we are not alone on this journey.

Music has a way of lifting our spirits and opening our hearts to Jesus' comfort and love. Turn on some worship music today and sing along as you praise God for His unfailing love and goodness.

DAY 162

"Teach me to do your will, for you are my God; may your good Spirit lead me on level ground."

Psalm 143:10

Are we seeking to do the will of God in everything we do? Or, do we get so caught up in thinking about what our child is doing or not doing that we forget about our own attitudes and actions. Most of our prayers revolve around asking God to change our child instead of seeking the ways in which He wants to lead us. Perhaps spending more time seeking God's will for ourselves will give us some new tools for coping with our child.

Spend time praying this Psalm today. Seek God's will in your life.

DAY 163

"The Lord will guide you always; he will satisfy your needs in a sun-scorched land and will strengthen your frame. You will be like a well-watered garden, like a spring whose waters never fail."

Isaiah 58:11

The contrast between a sun-scorched land and a well-watered garden is vivid, isn't it? Most of us would say we would choose the well-watered garden, but yet we remain stuck in the sun-scorched land. The good news is that we do have a choice! If we choose to allow the Lord to guide us, our needs will be met and He will help us move out of the desert and into the garden.

Surrender your path to the Lord today. Allow Him to strengthen you and lead you so that you can experience freedom from the desert and begin to enjoy all of the good things that He is waiting to give you.

"Blessed are those who keep his statutes and seek him with all their heart."

Psalm 119:2

One of the definitions of the word blessed is giving pleasure or contentment to the mind or senses. For some of us it has been awhile since we experienced pleasure because we are so consumed with our heartbreak over our child. This verse reminds us that our pleasure will come from the Lord if we earnestly seek Him. That means that we actively pursue or search for Him throughout our day.

Take your focus off of your child today so that you can earnestly seek the Lord and His will for you. You will be blessed.

DAY 165

"Let us not become weary in doing good, for at the proper time we will reap a harvest if we do not give up."

Galatians 6:9

Giving up is a constant temptation. When we are hurt, anxious, fearful, and even angry, it is pretty hard to "do good". However, we cannot let the choices of our child determine what our lives will be or how we will act. When we are consistent in doing good, no matter what is going on around us, we will eventually be rewarded.

Don't give up! Stay positive and ask God to help you to do good throughout this entire day.

DAY 166

"Always be joyful. Never stop praying. Be thankful in all circumstances, for this is God's will for you who belong to Christ Jesus."

1 Thessalonians 5:16-18 (NLT)

We know that God's will is for us to have joy in Christ Jesus, but joy is something that completely eludes us in the midst of our heartache over our child. The secret to experiencing joy, even in the midst of our struggle, is to "pray continually" and to give thanks for the good things in our lives. This verse says to give thanks in ALL circumstances, not just when things are going good.

Think about the good things in your life and spend time in prayer thanking God for them. Pay attention to how much better you feel right away. By doing this on a regular basis you will begin to experience joy again.

DAY 167

"Nothing in all creation is hidden from God's sight. Everything is uncovered and laid bare before the eyes of him to whom we must give account."

Hebrews 4:13

We sometimes feel like God has forgotten about us and our children. Doesn't He see what is going on? Does He even care? Scripture tells us that nothing is hidden from God's sight. He sees what is happening and He cares deeply because He loves us and He loves our kids. The important thing is how we handle ourselves while we are going through it. That is the one thing we have some control over. Are we acting in a way that honors God? Or are we allowing our pain to derail our faith?

Commit to honoring God with your own life, no matter what is going on with your child today. Make a conscious decision to place your trust in Him.

DAY 168

"I will search for the lost and bring back the strays. I will bind up the injured and strengthen the weak," says the Lord.

Ezekiel 34:16a

This verse speaks to us, not only because our children are lost, but because we are injured and weak. The Lord tells us that He will search for and bring our kids back as well as heal our pain while giving us strength. It is comforting to know that God does not give up on our kids. He continues to search for them with the intention of bringing them back. And in the meanwhile, He gives us the strength we need to carry on with our own lives.

Thank God for His steadfastness and love today. Rely on Him for your healing and strength.

DAY 169

"May our Lord Jesus Christ himself and God our Father, who loved us and by his grace gave us eternal encouragement and good hope, encourage your hearts and strengthen you in every good deed and word."

2 Thessalonians 2:16-17

We read about it over and over again in the Bible. God loves us and it is by His grace that we are encouraged, given hope and strengthened in spite of our own sin and the sin of our children. If we remember how much God loves us and our children and put our hope in Jesus we will not be disappointed. On the other hand, if our hope, joy and peace continue to be based on what is going on with our child, it is highly unlikely that our expectations for a peaceful and joy filled life will be met.

Focus on God's love today and allow Him to encourage you and give you hope.

DAY 170

"May you be richly rewarded by the Lord, the God of Israel, under whose wings you have come to take refuge."

Ruth 2:12b

Refuge means shelter or protection from danger or distress. The distress we feel can be totally overwhelming, but how awesome it is to know that we can take refuge "under the wings" of our loving Father. And guess what! He doesn't just want to protect us, He wants to richly reward us with a sense of wellbeing and peace as well.

Seek protection from your anxiety and pain in the arms (or under the wings) of the Father who created you and loves you enough to reward you richly, even in the midst of the turmoil.

DAY 171

"Observe what the Lord your God requires: Walk in obedience to him, and keep his decrees and commands, his laws and requirements . . . so that you may prosper in all you do and wherever you go."

1 Kings 2:3

Sometimes we get so caught up in trying to control our children and worrying about what they are doing or not doing that we forget to pay attention to how we are conducting our own lives. We may have forgotten about walking in the ways of the Lord and perhaps somewhere along the way we stopped earnestly seeking His will.

Are your thoughts and actions consistent with the ways of the Lord? Do you have an area of disobedience in your life? Ask God for forgiveness and move forward with a new resolve to seek God and to draw closer to Him.

DAY 172

"Therefore, my friends, I want you to know that through Jesus the forgiveness of sins is proclaimed to you."

Acts 13:38

Because we are human we all have sin in our lives. We carry guilt for our sin causing us to blame ourselves for what is happening with our child and we feel that we have failed as a parent. The good news is that Jesus already paid the price for our sin and we have been forgiven. It is only once we are able to forgive ourselves and let go of our guilt that we can begin to move beyond our pain.

Accept God's forgiveness and ask him to help you to forgive yourself for the sin in your life.

DAY 173

"Those whom I love I rebuke and discipline".

Revelation 3:19a

We often feel intimidated by our wayward child. We don't want to rock the boat with them and we are afraid to speak up, especially when they are behaving in a way that causes us anxiety and discomfort in our own home. This verse reminds us that when we love someone we can and should rebuke and discipline them.

Ask God to give you the courage and strength to communicate with your child in a way that will express your true feelings without causing you to feel fearful or anxious.

DAY 174

"And this hope will not lead to disappointment. For we know how dearly God loves us, because he has given us the Holy Spirit to fill our hearts with his love."

Romans 5:5 (NLT)

If we are placing our hope in our child's behavior we are going to be very disappointed. Our hope should always be in the God who loves us and our kids so much that He has given us the Holy Spirit to guide and direct us as well as fill our hearts with love. We will not be disappointed if our hope is in Him.

Focus on the love of God. Be aware of the Holy Spirit in your life today and allow Him to fill the places where you have been experiencing disappointment.

DAY 175

"The Lord is my light and my salvation—whom shall I fear? The Lord is the stronghold of my life—of whom shall I be afraid?"

Psalm 27:1

It is so easy to forget that the Lord is the one who gives us what we need to get through each day. We don't have to be afraid of what is going to happen next because He is in control. When everything seems dark and foreboding we need to remember that He will light the way for us. It's all about faith, and when we make the choice to trust God with our own lives as well as with our child we can move forward to the life He has planned for us.

Make a conscious choice to trust God. Allow Him to light the way for you as you navigate through this day.

DAY 176

"All Scripture is God-breathed and is useful for teaching, rebuking, correcting and training in righteousness so that the servant of God may be thoroughly equipped for every good work."

2 Timothy 3:16-17

We feel so ill-equipped to deal with the things that are coming our way through our child right now. This isn't what we signed up for when we became a parent. Our dreams for our child are being shattered and we have no idea what to say, how to act, or even how to think. The Bible is our handbook for life and will give us some of the answers we are seeking. Scripture is God-breathed by the same God who created us and our kids and we can trust that what we read is true and right.

Open your Bible today and seek the comfort and the wisdom that you long for.

DAY 177

"My flesh and my heart may fail, but God is the strength of my heart and my portion forever."

Psalm 73:26

On our own we cannot manage or control the anguish we are experiencing. Our hearts are broken and we lash out in ways that are not helpful and cause us shame. God is the one who can heal our hearts and give us the strength to handle ourselves in a way that will not add to the pain that we already have. When we are out of control, He is in control. When we are weak, He is strong.

Commit to allowing God to take control of your life today. He will begin to mend your heart.

DAY 178

"Anyone who believes in him will never be put to shame."

Romans 10:11b

Having a child who is out of control and doing things that are damaging and destructive causes us to be ashamed. Everyone else seems to have perfect kids and we are just sure that other people are judging us. We begin to believe that the actions of our child are our fault and we feel as though we have failed as a parent. If we believe what the Bible tells us about the love of Jesus and we accept what He did for us when He died on the cross, we do not have to feel ashamed. Jesus paid the price for all our sins.

Surrender any shame you have today and seek to identify with the ways that you are loved and valued through Jesus.

DAY 179

"Yet now I am happy, not because you were made sorry, but because your sorrow led you to repentance."

2 Corinthians 7:9a

These were the Apostle Paul's words to the people in the church in Corinth and they can definitely apply to us today. When we are suffering because our hearts are broken, we don't know where else to turn and so we turn to God. We come to the end of ourselves and realize that we don't have the answers, and the things that are hurting us are out of our control. To repent means to turn. We repent by turning away from our old way of doing things and allowing God to give us a new way.

Repent today. Turn to God and allow Him to start the process of mending your heart.

DAY 180

"May your unfailing love be with us, Lord, even as we put our hope in you."

Psalm 33:22

We have been disappointed over and over again because we keep hoping that our child will turn around. We grab on to even the slightest sign that they might be changing, and our spirits are lifted for a moment only to come crashing down again when nothing happens. Day by day, moment by moment, our focus is on our child and the negative and damaging choices they are making. This verse reminds us to put our hope in the Lord. His unfailing love can give us the encouragement we so desperately need.

Be aware of God's amazing love today and allow yourself to be encouraged by Him.

DAY 181

"Lift your eyes and look to the heavens: Who created all these? He who brings out the starry host one by one and calls them each by name. Because of his great power and mighty strength, not one of them is missing."

Isaiah 40:26

We sometimes feel like God has forgotten about our child and has surely forgotten about us. But if God has created every star and calls each of them by name, He is certainly powerful enough to remember us, His precious children, whom He has created in the image of Himself. It's up to us to turn to Him and allow Him to be our refuge, while we trust Him with the outcome of our situation, no matter what it is.

Be confident in the fact that God is totally aware of you and your child and He is waiting for you to lay your grief and your pain at His feet. Surrender your situation to Him today so that you can begin to heal.

DAY 182

"He has made everything beautiful in its time. He has also set eternity in the human heart; yet no one can fathom what God has done from beginning to end."

Ecclesiastes 3:11

God is good! He deals in beauty, grace, redemption, and restoration. We get frustrated because we can't see the big picture; we don't know what lies ahead. Our time on earth is miniscule compared to eternity and we cannot possibly know what the entire big picture looks like. Only God knows what has been, what is to come, and how it all works together. But because we know that God is good and He loves us, we can trust that He is working to make everything beautiful, even when we can't see it.

Has there been a time in your life when you recognized God's hand in resolving a situation that you thought was impossible? Think about times like that today and thank Him for His faithfulness then, now, and in the future.

DAY 183

"Watch and pray so that you will not fall into temptation. The spirit is willing, but the flesh is weak."

Matthew 26:41

We are desperate for freedom from the constant worry and anxiety we are experiencing. We have good intentions when we surrender our child to God. But the temptation to try to fix and control them is so great, that despite our decision to let go, we continuously find ourselves right back where we started. It is our own weakness that often causes us the most grief because we don't stick with our plan of allowing God to be the one to handle our child.

Remember this Scripture throughout your day today. Surrender your child to God and then "watch and pray" so that you will have the strength to remain committed to trusting God and letting Him be in control.

DAY 184

"Let all who take refuge in God be glad; let them ever sing for joy. Spread your protection over them, that those who love your name may rejoice in you."

Psalm 5:11

Sometimes we look for refuge from our stress and pain in things that drive us farther from the Lord, who is the only one who can truly protect us and give us joy again. We sleep, or shop, or drink, or work, anything to mask how we are feeling. But in the long run, those things only prolong and intensify the negative emotions that are just below the surface.

Take refuge in the Lord today by praising Him for the good things in your life. Allow Him to protect you from your pain and begin to experience the joy that He will give you in spite of what is going on with your child.

DAY 185

"The Lord your God is with you, the Mighty Warrior who saves. He will take great delight in you; in his love he will no longer rebuke you, but will rejoice over you with singing."

Zephaniah 3:17

We may not be able to sense God's presence because we are so caught up in worry, frustration, and disappointment over our child. However, this verse assures us the He is with us and He wants to save us from our pain. His love is enough to quiet our hearts, and just as we want to be able to take delight in our kids again, that is exactly what God wants to do with us! We are His kids.

Open yourself up to God's love today by acknowledging that He is with you. Allow His presence and His love to quiet your broken heart.

DAY 186

"Hear my cry, O God; listen to my prayer. From the ends of the earth I call to you, I call as my heart grows faint; lead me to the rock that is higher than I. For you have been my refuge, a strong tower against the foe. I long to dwell in your tent forever and take refuge in the shelter of your wings."

Psalm 61:1-4

As day after day, month after month, and year after year go by we begin to lose hope that our child will ever turn around. Although we have cried out and prayed for them for so long, we are unable to see God working in our child's life and our faith begins to waiver. But perhaps in our desperate desire to have our child change we have lost sight of what God might be trying to do in our own lives. Maybe we have forgotten to allow Him to lead us "to the rock that is higher than I" and to take refuge in Him.

Spend some time today seeking God's will for your own life. Draw closer to Him and allow Him to lead you.

DAY 187

"But you, dear friends, by building yourselves up in your most holy faith and praying in the Holy Spirit, keep yourselves in God's love as you wait for the mercy of our Lord Jesus Christ to bring you to eternal life."

Jude 1:20-21

If we will transfer our energy from worrying about our child to building up our own faith in Jesus we will feel a lot better. God's love is all around us and it is so comforting to know that we can tap into it at any time.

When you feel yourself getting anxious today, turn to God in prayer and thank Him for His love and His mercy. Ask Him to strengthen your faith and expect Him to replace your anxiety with His perfect peace.

DAY 188

"Do not be afraid, for I am with you; I will bring your children from the east and gather you from the west. I will say to the north, 'Give them up!' and to the south, 'Do not hold them back.' Bring my sons from afar and my daughters from the ends of the earth."

Isaiah 43:5-6

God wants to save our kids because, remember, they are His sons and daughters too. He doesn't want us to be afraid because not only is He with us, but He is working to bring our kids back. He gives them the freedom to choose, just as He does with us, but He is constantly trying to get their attention. We can't change our kids and we can't be the ones to turn them around. But when we feel like we need to be "doing" something, we can stand in the gap and pray for them.

Spend some time in prayer for your child today. Pray that the situations that God is orchestrating to get their attention will be effective and that they will begin to understand the depth of His love for them.

DAY 189

"And this is love: that we walk in obedience to his commands. As you have heard from the beginning, his command is that you walk in love."

2 John 1:6

Are you walking in obedience to God by walking in love? Or are you walking in bitterness, anger, and resentment because you are allowing your child's actions to cause you so much heartache? The good news is that we have a choice. We can choose to walk in love with the strength and help of God.

Ask God to help you to walk in love throughout your day. Express to Him your desire to be obedient in your thoughts, words, and actions.

DAY 190

"Let your light shine before others, that they may see your good deeds and glorify your Father in heaven."

Matthew 5:16b

As we begin to heal and recognize that we are having better days, we can be the ones to offer hope to someone else who is devastated over their child. God never wastes a hurt and as He restores us, and we share the story of what He has done in our lives, we will be a light to others who are in a place of despair.

Don't be afraid to share your story. Allow someone else to see what God is doing in your life by sharing where you have been and how He has begun to heal and restore you.

DAY 191

"For God so loved the world that he gave his one and only Son, that whoever believes in him shall not perish but have eternal life."

John 3:16

God loves us so much that He sent His only son, who sacrificed His own life for ours. He loves our kids that much too and it is His desire that they would believe in Him and not perish. Isn't that our greatest fear? That our child will perish because of the way they are living? It is comforting to know that God wants the same things for our child that we want.

Surrender your child to the God who loves them enough to sacrifice His only son for them. At the same time, allow Him to work in your own life, giving you wisdom, strength and peace.

DAY 192

"Whoever dwells in the shelter of the Most High will rest in the shadow of the Almighty."

Psalm 91:1

To dwell in the shelter of the Most High means to get as close as we possibly can to God. When we are walking next to Him every hour of every day we will be protected from the anxiety and fear that threaten to consume us when we are alone. As we learn to trust Him we can rest knowing He is in control. We can be closer to Him through prayer, meditation, Bible reading, and spending time in nature.

Draw closer to God today by spending some quality time with Him.

DAY 193

"We have confidence before God and receive from him anything we ask, because we keep his commands and do what pleases him."

1 John 3:21b-22

We have prayed our hearts out, and still nothing seems to be changing with our child. But, we don't know how God might be using the circumstances surrounding them to bring about change. Scripture tells us that we can trust "in confidence" that He is in the process of answering our prayers. On the other hand, are we obeying His commands and living our own lives in a way that pleases Him? Perhaps it is time for us to focus on how we can be the women God has designed us to be by being obedient and striving to please Him with our own lives.

Spend time today seeking God's commands for yourself and asking Him to help you be obedient.

DAY 194

"You will call on me and come and pray to me, and I will listen to you. You will seek me and find me when you seek me with all your heart," says the Lord.

Jeremiah 29:12-13

Instead of focusing on begging God to fix our children, we should instead seek what His commands are for us so that we can be obedient in our own lives. This verse assures us that when we earnestly seek Him we will find Him and He will listen to us. This painful time in our lives is an opportunity for us to draw closer to God and to experience His goodness. Let's not be so caught up in worry about our kids that we miss out on the good things that He has for us.

Continue seeking God today. Spend time seeking him with "all your heart" and know that He is listening to you.

DAY 195

"So we fix our eyes not on what is seen, but on what is unseen, since what is seen is temporary, but what is unseen is eternal."

2 Corinthians 4:18

It is somehow comforting to remember that as painful as this time in our lives is, and as long as it is lasting, it is not permanent. We can't see beyond this year or even this day, but the bottom line is that this life on earth, with all of its sorrow and pain, is temporary. The pain-free life that we seek is going to be a reality in Heaven with God, and that life is forever—eternal.

Spend some time imagining a pain-free life in the presence of the Father who loves you. What will that look like for you?

"*Love is patient, love is kind. It does not envy, it does not boast, it is not proud. It does not dishonor others, it is not self-seeking, it is not easily angered, it keeps no record of wrongs. Love does not delight in evil but rejoices with the truth. It always protects, always trusts, always hopes, and always perseveres.*"

1 Corinthians 13:4-7

DAY 196

These verses in 1 Corinthians are part of what is known as "The Love Chapter" of the Bible. It tells us what love looks like and gives us guidelines for how to love others.

Today, instead of thinking about all of the negative things that your child is doing, meditate on these words and remember how to love them in the midst of this struggle. It is also a good reminder of how we should be loving the other members of our family. So often we allow our pain and anxiety to get in the way of loving other people near us in the way that they deserved to be loved – in the way that God wants us to love them.

DAY 197

"Do not conform to the pattern of this world, but be transformed by the renewing of your mind. Then you will be able to test and approve what God's will is—his good, pleasing and perfect will."

Romans 12:2

When we conform to the pattern of this world we allow external forces, such as the behavior of our child, to dictate what our attitude will be. We allow anger, bitterness, anxiety and fear to burrow in and take over. But God's will for us is good and does not include these negative and debilitating emotions.

Allow Jesus to renew your mind today by reading your Bibles, praying, and focusing on Him. Ask Him to help you not to conform to the pattern of this world, but to live within His good, pleasing and perfect will.

DAY 198

"Do not judge, and you will not be judged? Do not condemn, and you will not be condemned. Forgive, and you will be forgiven."

Luke 6:37

We feel that other people are judging and condemning us because of the choices our child is making. We are ashamed and at the same time resentful and holding on to unforgiveness. But how many times do we judge others without really knowing what is going on in their lives or what obstacles they are facing? Who are the people in our lives that we are condemning?

Ask God to help you with your own judgmental and condemning attitude. Ask Him to help you to forgive others so that you may also be forgiven. Expect to experience freedom when you stop judging and condemning and begin to extend forgiveness to those who may have hurt you.

DAY 199

Jesus looked at them and said, "With man this is impossible, but not with God; all things are possible with God."

Mark 10:27

Have you come to the conclusion that nothing is ever going to change with your child? Have you given up hope? This short verse of scripture offers us some very powerful words of hope! Jesus Himself told us that ALL things are possible with God.

Don't lose hope. Don't give up praying for your child. ALL things, even your child turning around, are possible with God. He loves you and He loves your child and it is His desire that you and your child would have rich, full, peace and joy filled lives. Keep praying for your child and keep seeking God's will for your own life.

DAY 200

"But thanks be to God! He gives us the victory through our Lord Jesus Christ."

1 Corinthians 15:57

Because we are so focused on our child the only victory we can think about is for them to change and turn from their destructive behavior. However, could it be that the real victory is in what God wants to do in us? Isn't most of the battle that we are facing stemming from our own anxiety and fear? Perhaps the real victory is about moving beyond those emotions that are tearing us up and making our lives miserable. The Scriptures say that the victory can be ours through Jesus Christ.

Change your battle cry today and seek victory over your negative emotions, allowing Jesus to replace them with peace and joy.

I hope that reading these Words of Encouragement each day has brought you comfort and that you have come to understand just how much the God of the universe loves you and loves your child. He alone can give you everything you need to be the best woman and mom you can be. Allow Him to walk with you through this season of your life and trust Him to uphold you with the strength and courage you are seeking.

Remember, God is in control and we are not!

Cathy Taylor

Do you feel totally isolated and alone in your heartbreak over your child? Does it seem as though everyone else's kids are perfect? Do you long to share your struggles with other moms who know exactly what you are going through?

Hurting Moms, Mending Hearts is a community of women who know what it is like to have a child who is out of control, and making self-destructive choices. They've experienced the pain, anxiety, fear, and shame that happens to moms in this situation.

We encourage you join our community and connect with other Hurting Moms to find hope and healing. There is something very special that happens when moms who are suffering over their kids come together.

Online at Hurting Moms you will discover a community of moms just like yourself, as well as videos and other valuable resources to lift and encourage you.

Go to www.HurtingMoms.com and sign up for our online version of Daily Words of Encouragement.

YOU ARE NOT ALONE!

www.HurtingMoms.com